THE RIGHT MOVES

THE RIGHT MOVES

A Dancer's Training

DAPHNE HURFORD

THE ATLANTIC MONTHLY PRESS
New York

Library of Congress Cataloging-in-Publication Data

Hurford, Daphne.
  The right moves.

  I. Title.
PS3558.U5327R5   1987   813'.54   87-939
ISBN 0-87113-148-X

FIRST EDITION

Published simultaneously in Canada
Printed in the United States of America

Design by Laura Hough

For Sandy

Contents

Contents

Contents

List of Illustrations

THE RIGHT MOVES

I.

Blowup

According to Max, Josh had called him a little fucker. Josh insists he only said Max was stupid, but Max is adamant in his claim. He heard "little fucker." It was one of those soft, early spring days; the air was dizzy with promises. The boys would soon be sixteen, both of them. A glance out the huge, high windows of the studio at the late-afternoon light shimmering down Broadway confirmed that the days were stretching out, lengthening. The dozen or so teenage boys inside the room were trying to get the same effect with their arms, legs, and torsos. They spilled across the floor, bending and reaching, working knots out of muscles, coaxing tendons into pliability. They could have been preparing for a football or baseball game except for their tights and turned-out feet. It was a little after five P.M.; ballet class was to begin at five-thirty.

Krammie was the day's teacher. Andrei Kramarevsky is a big, Russian bear of a man who danced with the Bolshoi and is married to a Russian circus alumna. His English is sparse, his body language eloquent. Giant blue eyes roll about in his rosy face. His mobile mouth turns up or down with equal dexterity, and excitement engages his entire body—arms

3

gesture, trunk bends, legs cave in at the knees. Krammie is a true Muscovite; bravura Bolshoi is his basic balletic nature.

His voice resounds throughout the fifty-foot-long studio. "Te*rrrr*ible," he will groan, *r*'s rolling. "Deesgustink!" "Sm*iiii*le," he will exhort, grinning. "Nut baddh," he will judge work well done. When inspiring his students to give that extra measure, to add their own personal verve to the age-old steps, he tells them to make it look "Ex*penseee*ve!" Often he is clad in a T-shirt that bears the inscription, "Expensive but worth it."

The boys are always glad for Krammie's class; it's their chance to hurl themselves about the room, to leap and spin and try the terrifying tricks with which they plan to dazzle audiences when they become stars. It is also their chance to blow off some of the steam that otherwise only builds up day after day, class after class, week after week.

But first, though, before any leaps or spins or even mini-tricks, there is the half hour of basics—even in Krammie's class—repeating and repeating the small, controlled movements out of which classical dance is made, holding on to the wooden barre that dissects three walls of the room. These are the ABC's of ballet, Terpsichore's times tables; they convince the body and the brain to cooperate with each other. Barre work engages the entire body; it is said to be the most complete workout imaginable. It is demanding, difficult, frustrating, "b*ooo*ring."

That early spring day Max had had a head start in the frustration department. He was, as they say, "loaded for bear." He had seen Josh in the dressing room before class. They didn't speak, but one glimpse was enough to fuel his fury. He had heard that Josh had been saying nasty things about him, telling people that Max's mother was a bitch, that

Max was a woman, a faggot. A chip as big as a house had been built up on Max's shoulder; it was just begging to be jostled. He says all he could think was, "if he just looks at me the wrong way . . . if he gives me any reason at all . . ."

The barre work was over. The piano had been moved to the corner; the students would now take over the whole space. Krammie divided them into two groups, then demonstrated a combination of steps. The pianist played and played; the first group of boys tried the steps four or five times, with Krammie commenting and correcting; then they cleared the floor so the second batch could have a chance. The combinations were hard, physically and mentally taxing. The room was getting hotter and hotter, stuffier and stuffier; boys were panting and sweating. Max crossed the floor, walked to the door and opened it, then rejoined his group to await his turn. Then he danced. While he was doing the steps Josh strode over and closed the door. Max finished and, trying to look casual, sauntered over and opened it. Josh started to close the door again. It was a classic standoff, and Max says he thought, "This is my chance. I just know it." All his frustration since he had moved to New York and come to this school, all his confusion, his disappointment at not doing better, at not being a favorite, all his rage bubbled up and focused on Josh. It was as though Josh had a bull's-eye painted on his chin.

Through clenched teeth Max ordered Josh to leave the door open. Josh responded either, "Don't be stupid," or "You little fucker," and the place exploded. Max slammed his fist into Josh's face as hard as he could, gashing open his lower lip. Flailing, Josh struck back, then spat a mouthful of blood over Max. The rest of the boys petrified into statues where they stood. Krammie raced about, wringing his hands and crying out: "No! Boy*ssss*! Pl*eeess*! Ballet, boy*sss*! Don't h*eet*! Ballet!" Josh stormed out of the room and was quickly intercepted by a teacher who got him some ice and delivered him to the school office.

In the studio Max began to panic. "Oh, my God, what have I done?" was his first thought, he says. Then he calmed down. "I don't care," he decided. "Whatever happens, happens. I'm glad I did it." He tore into the dressing room, though, hoping to grab his clothes and make a hasty exit. He gathered torn sweats on over his tights, threw on his sneakers and his brother's Highland Park High School letter jacket, and ran. He almost made it, but not quite. Feeling his freedom within easy reach, Max rushed out into the hall . . . smack into Krammie, Josh, and Sinikka Finn, the school receptionist and the administrative person-in-charge during these early evening hours. They all looked at Max as though he had been created in some mad scientist's laboratory. Furiously Ms. Finn ordered, "Max, go back into the dressing room, clear out your locker, and go home. Tomorrow morning report to Mrs. Gleboff!" Krammie just shook his head sadly; Josh looked triumphant.

Humiliation, fear, and an odd exhilaration collided in Max as he emptied his locker, scooping out dirty clothes, torn slippers, and, at the bottom, the paperback fantasy novel he'd spent weeks looking for. He flew down the two flights of stairs and out onto the sidewalk. The door closed behind him, and he was stung by the gray darkness and damp chill. All traces of spring were gone; with them went his joy and confidence. What would happen now? How could he tell his mother? What would she do? What would *they* do? Suddenly this turned into the worst day in Max's decade and a half on earth . . . worse than his first days in New York, and worse even than the day last summer when he'd had his hip operation. Would they kick him out? Would he and his mother and sister have to go back to Texas in defeat? Would they stay and make him go back alone to live with his father? That's what his mother always threatened when nothing else worked. That was her trump card, but would she actually do it? The thought was intolerable. It wasn't that Pappy was so bad; he wasn't. It was that Max couldn't leave New York, he just couldn't, and he wouldn't . . . but what would he do?

He got off the bus at Eighty-eighth and Broadway and trudged the block and a half to his building. His feet, those

Max, pre-blowup, outside New York's Lincoln Center.

prized appendages he was training to be strong and light and supple, were leaden and clumsy. His shoulders slumped over; his neck lurched forward as though Mrs. Gleboff's hand were on it. Max had met his enemy, and he was it.

Max often lied to his mother. He told her what he thought she wanted to hear and left out anything he thought she wouldn't like. He made up things to tell her too. It was easier that way. This time it wouldn't work; this time he knew he had to face the facts and face her wrath. He was terrified. The minute he saw her, he blurted out his tale, then prepared for her onslaught. They had had an impossible year together. He thought she was too strict; she thought he was too fresh. The stricter she got, the more defiant he became. Both had tempers, hot Texas tempers, and their voices were often raised. This time, though, Brenda Fuqua just listened quietly to her son. Then she was silent for a minute or two. When she finally spoke, Max was astonished to learn that she was not going to hold any of their earlier struggles against him. No. Instead she shifted into full gear and directed all her copious energies toward protecting his status as a would-be ballet dancer. And hers as his mother.

Max's mother had no intention of going back to Dallas, either. She told Max to leave the next day's meeting to her; then she started to map out her plan of attack on that small Russian citadel known as Mrs. Gleboff.

Also, as an insurance policy, in case Max actually were thrown out, she made a list of all the other ballet schools and teachers she thought to be worthwhile. There was Richard Thomas; there was David Howard; there was Robert Joffrey. Maybe one of them would take Max. He wouldn't ever be able to join the New York City Ballet now, but there were other companies. American Ballet Theatre might accept him.

Or perhaps they should move . . . maybe to England. She'd always wanted to live there. Peter Schaufuss was the director of the London Festival Ballet. He'd be a great teacher, she thought. Her mind churned full speed ahead. Urgently. Then she slowed down. No. No. No. The School of American Ballet was where Max was now. It was the most prestigious of all the schools; it was where he belonged. She'd just have to convince Mrs. Gleboff, the school's executive director, to keep him. She wasn't sure how she was going to do it, but she was. Somehow. It couldn't all fall apart now; she wouldn't let it.

Despite her brave front, Brenda was frightened. Max had been as big a pain at school the past year as he was at home. He had skipped class regularly, defied the strict dress code daily, and basically been indolent, much preferring to hang around the hall smoking cigarettes and flirting with the budding ballerinas—being "cool"—to the actual hard work required of him. And what on earth would they do if he were expelled?

SAB, as the School of American Ballet is called, is the finest ballet academy in the United States; in fact, students come there from all over the world. The school is affiliated with the New York City Ballet (not American Ballet Theatre, as might be assumed from its name). This is the school that Balanchine built, the result of his legendary response—"But first, a school"—to Lincoln Kirstein's invitation to found a ballet company on these shores. Since SAB opened its doors in January of 1934, the school has trained just about all the top American balletic talent and supplied companies around the world with highly skilled dancers. Over its half century plus, SAB has grown enormously—in size, stature, and endowment. Today it is as close to a national ballet academy as our democratic system permits.

The teachers at SAB come from Imperial Russia, Soviet Russia, Europe, and the United States. They share a devotion to their craft and a common goal—producing the finest possible classical dancers. If Russian or Danish or English is their balletic mother tongue, they have all also learned to speak Balanchine, for it is this master's vision that is the overriding artistic influence of the school. All of ballet is an amalgam. The Danish master Bournonville was trained in France; the Russian master Petipa moved from Paris to choreograph for the czar. George Balanchine was born in Russia, but he studied with the Italian master Cecchetti when both were in Paris, and he also spent time as ballet master for the Royal Danish company. Each, in his own time and to his own ability, takes all that has come before, adds his own inspiration to the mix, and brings ballet a step ahead of where it was, enlarges and enhances the possibilities of classical dance. SAB students learn the same elements that Russian, Danish, and British students learn, but they are also imbued with the most up-to-date, state-of-the-art, neoclassical vision of Mr. B., even though most of them are too young ever to have met the maestro, and plenty aren't really sure just who he was, anyhow.

It's harder to "dance Balanchine" than any other way. Neoclassicism demands that every movement be larger, faster, more explicit, and more defined than any style that preceded it. These young acolytes work, in each one-and-one-half-hour class at SAB, more intensely and more vigorously than do their counterparts at any other school.

There are three men who teach regularly at SAB: the Russian Krammie, the Anglo-Dane Stanley Williams, and the American Richard Rapp. Others come in from time to time, and the Boss, Peter Martins, conducts an occasional class; but

Williams, Kramarevsky, and Rapp form the backbone of male instruction available at the school. Except for the very youngest, the eight- and nine-year-olds, SAB boys take class only with boys and study only with men. They rehearse for performances with the female teachers, and they are influenced by them, but all their classes are taught by one of the three vastly different men. Balanchine insisted it be that way. Demonstration is a vital part of any ballet class: Description can only go so far, and students must be able to see what it is that is being asked of them. It is, after all, a highly visual discipline. Balanchine believed that boys must always have male role models, must see men demonstrating the correct arm position, for instance, so that they will learn to use their bodies in the specific ways that danseurs should, so that they will become embodiments of masculine dancing. Many of the steps for boys are the same as those for girls, but the philosophy is very, very different, and there is nothing worse than a boy who dances like a girl.

The older and most gifted students at SAB, the boys who are in the Advanced Men's and Special Men's classes, study with Krammie and Stanley Williams. Williams is a former Royal Danish star. He has been Peter Martins's teacher since 1958, and now he and Martins are codirectors of faculty at SAB. In his autobiography, *Far From Denmark*, Martins has written, "Stanley became my teacher when I was 12. . . . It was Stanley Williams who made me feel the challenge, the potential achievement, the *importance* of being a dancer." Over the more than two decades that he has taught at SAB, Williams has become the mentor of just about every famous male star you can name, including Mikhail Baryshnikov. He has also been carefully, painstakingly, devotedly bringing back the young dazzler Darci Kistler from surgery that would have ended most careers. Soft-spoken and impeccably groomed, Williams teaches a class that is all but impossible for newcomers to understand. He speaks very little, and then never in whole sentences, only fragments, and very softly, abstractly, in a sort of balletic haiku that is fleshed out with elegant gestures. He says things like, "When you turn, just use your front; don't use your back." Or, "It's just the opposite of what you think," and he is often heard correcting imperfections by saying, "You see, you do this, but I do that," the *this* and *that* imperceptibly, but vitally, different. One of his hands is usually wrapped around the bowl of a pipe he puffs on regularly. His gray, wavy hair is meticulously clipped and combed; his trousers look as though he never sits down, and his beautifully ironed pink or white or striped long-sleeved shirts, open at the neck, don't dare to wrinkle. There is nothing stiff and rigid about Stanley, though; it's just that he's a perfectionist, a calm and patient one, a gently obsessed passer-on of the flame ignited by August Bournonville.

Boys who take Stanley's class often get to share barre space with their heroes. Baryshnikov takes Stanley's class when he's in New York; so does Nureyev. When Martins and Misha were both dancing with the New York City Ballet, the kids in Advanced got to see a little high-level sibling rivalry as the two competed for Stanley's approval. One day Studio 3 contained five of the greatest male dancers alive scattered among the students—Martins, Baryshnikov, Nureyev, Helgi Tomasson, and Fernando Bujones. Peter and Misha were really going at it, avidly playing "Can you top this?" Stanley is not easy to impress; tricks alone don't do it. Perfect technique is what it takes, artistry. Barre was over, and the students had moved to the center of the room. The combination ended with a pirouette. Most of the students did two. Bujones did

Stanley Williams, teaching Advanced Men's class at SAB.

four, ending beautifully; Martins added one more and a slightly more perfect stop. Suddenly Baryshnikov ripped off thirteen—yes, thirteen—consecutive three-hundred-sixty-degree turns, spinning like a dervish. He finished his super-human feat and looked to Stanley for a big smile and a kind word. Stanley was impassive. He took a small pull on his pipe, nodded a couple of times, looked long at the Russian, and said gently, "That's very nice, Misha. But . . . you know, . . . it's not ballet." The star took his place among the students, and class resumed.

The Intermediate and younger boys at SAB study with Krammie and Richard Rapp. All the boys call Stanley "Stanley," and Krammie "Krammie." They call Richard "Mr. Rapp." One senses that if Richard Rapp weren't a gifted dancer turned teacher of dance, he would be a gifted physicist turned teacher of physics. He's a natural educator, calm,

13

clear, and logical, and he began teaching dance when he was still a student himself. Richard Rapp is a Midwesterner, having grown up on the western shores of Lake Michigan, in Milwaukee, and he's as American as Krammie is Russian. He started off as a tap dancer and was lured into ballet by his cousin, who needed a partner. For the first ten classes he took, he refused to don tights. Then he got to Chicago, saw the Ballet Russe de Monte Carlo, and thought, "I just know I

Krammie:
Expensive but
worth it.

Sherrie Nickol

14

can do that." He was right, and he was hooked. Although the United States Army interrupted his progress, he joined the New York City Ballet in 1956 and enjoyed a distinguished sixteen-year career there, achieving the rank of soloist.

Rapp and Krammie are Max's teachers, and they are as different from each other as possible. As ebullient, outgoing, and sketched with wide, bold brush strokes as Krammie is, Rapp is contained, controlled, authoritative, a fine-grade pen-

Sherrie Nickol

Richard Rapp, training the Intermediate men.

15

and-pencil drawing. He is a purist and an avid Balanchine believer. He can be heard admonishing a class that is having some collective difficulty assimilating corrections, "This is the way Mr. Balanchine wanted it done, and he knew a great deal more about ballet than we do. So let's do it his way." Mr. Rapp is of middle height and smallish build. His copper-lighted hair is easing the way for his skull to shine through, but his luxurious mustache is full, flourishing, and untouched by gray. Krammie is apt to cover his barrel chest with inscribed T-shirts or glitzy net creations to teach in; Mr. Rapp wears his own version of work clothes—striped short-sleeved golf shirts and bell-bottom trousers. Krammie strides around in Adidas or Nike sneakers; Mr. Rapp's amazingly arched feet are always encased in proper ballet slippers. He's a quiet man, intelligent and thoughtful, endowed with a wry and occasionally caustic wit. He can be gentle, nurturing, as patient as a saint, and he can also be startlingly blunt.

When things are not going so well in class, Stanley will stop the pianist and softly say, seeming incredulous that this misunderstanding could exist, "No. Boys? No." Then he will start all over again, expecting they will see the error of their ways. Krammie will bellow, "Vot? Yech! Deeesgustink!" Everyone will have a chuckle, and on they will go. Mr. Rapp will clap his hands lightly to stop the boys and the music, single out the offender, and coldly query, "Have you decided that this is the way you are going to dance for the rest of your life? If so, just tell me and I'll stop bothering you." The chagrined student mutters an all but inaudible "No," and the teacher responds, "Good. Then I still have a chance." And things return to normal.

II.

Close Call

Regularly at SAB there is one male who doesn't teach class, though everyone there learns from him all the time. Lincoln Kirstein is the president and cofounder of the school. It was he who brought Balanchine to America. He was but twenty-six years old when he met the Russian in Paris in 1933 and wrote home to his friend Chick Austin, director of the Hartford, Connecticut, Athenaeum, saying: "This will be the most important letter I will ever write you. . . . My pen burns my hand as I write. . . . We have a real chance to have an American ballet within three years' time. When I say ballet, I mean a trained company of young dancers, not Russians, but Americans with Russian stars to start with. . . . Do you know Georges Balanchine? If not, he is a Georgian called Georgi Balanchivadze. He is personally enchanting—dark, very slight, a superb dancer and the most ingenious technician I have ever seen. . . ."

Due to Kirstein's insistence, invention, and infusion of funds, the School of American Ballet came into existence. Without him the school wouldn't have happened; the New York City Ballet wouldn't have happened. Ballet

17

American-style wouldn't have happened. Kirstein has often been described as a moral presence at SAB; it's an accurate description.

He is a big man, tall with wide shoulders and a studied and stunning appearance. His hair and complexion are pale and slightly translucent. He dresses always in a black suit, white shirt, and narrow black tie (except for occasional summer evenings when he brings out his white flannels, navy blazer, and white leather shoes). His only adornment is a golden lyre pinned to his left lapel. It is the same pin that Georgi Balanchivadze wore as a child to signify that he was a dance student at the Imperial School in St. Petersburg.

Kirstein has a fierce demeanor, which seems calculated to fend off fools who might otherwise interrupt his progress and waste his time. His shoulders, neck, and head lunge forward slightly; his mouth is unsmiling, and his eyes are intense behind their glasses. One expects a gruff voice and is surprised to find it soft and rather high-pitched. A *New York Times* article once described a lunch Kirstein was having with some old friends. Suddenly he looked up at his companions, declared vehemently that they were just plain boring, and stomped away from the table, never to reappear. He can also be courtly, though, totally charming.

He is among the smartest men in America, but even he could not have known how well his megalomaniacal obsession as a young man would come to fruition. He planned nothing less than to establish an American balletic tradition, and he has done so. The United States is now the dance capital of the world, and Kirstein is the mason whose resources, material and other, laid the foundation upon which many others have built. Adults often fear or are in awe of Lincoln Kirstein, but not the tiny eight-year-old, berry-red-

Carolyn George

Lincoln Kirstein, SAB president, cofounder, and moral presence.

leotard-clad ballerinas whose heads he tousles as they rush by him on their way to class.

The dreaded Mrs. Gleboff, or Madame Gleboff, the executive director of SAB, is small, dark-haired, middle-aged but still somewhat girlish. Nathalie Gleboff has a pretty face and a calm, polite manner. Her voice is rich, Russian-accented, cultured. She's been with the school since 1959. When she smiles or laughs, her eyes crinkle, her head tilts backward, and her face lights up. But when she is serious, somber, or just official, her eyes are cool, strong, piercing, her manner old-worldly, formal. She is a force to be reckoned with. Nathalie Molostwoff, her predecessor, is still at the school as director emeritus. The women are known as the two Natashas. It falls to the younger Natasha to deliver news, good or bad, to pupils and parents alike. At the end of the school year she is the one who gives each student the teachers' assessment of progress or its lack. She is the one who tells of promotion to the next level; she also tells the unwanted they must leave. She is the one who breaks the news that breaks the heart, and she is also the one who must deal with any and all discipline problems.

And there are always discipline problems, or at least situations to be dealt with. Boys will be boys, after all, even if they regularly breathe the rarefied air of the world of ballet. And adolescence, that time of turmoil for even the dullest of us, is a watershed period for those whom George Balanchine called his Poets of Gesture. Hormones rage and bodies betray. "Pretty kittens can turn into horrid cats," says Kirstein, an avowed felinophile. Pounds ooze on or melt off. Height is either painfully lacking or added so fast that strength is lost. Boys are given a long grace period to see how their bodies will surprise them, but there is a not so subtle pressure for the little frogs to turn miraculously into tall, strong, coordinated, musical, and handsome princes. And outside interests beckon like sirens. The tedium of constant repetition, monastic discipline, and regular failure could discourage even the ever-cheerful Peter Pan, and there is little room for rebellion, adolescent or otherwise.

Madame Gleboff understands all this, but she also understands maintaining standards. Missed classes can quickly add up to suspension; wild or even artistically silk-screened T-shirts instead of the regulation white are viewed with similar skepticism. Attitude is assessed daily, but youth is given a measure of amnesty. The hallways of SAB, even when teeming with teenagers, are quieter than any academic

20

school. The boys' dressing room, however, is trashed yearly, holes poked in the ceiling, lockers broken, and walls smeared with bubble gum. For those infractions there is no serious reprisal. Stealing results in instant dismissal, no explanations invited or heard, but lesser transgressors are usually given a second or even a third try.

Unless the boy shows no dancing promise, that is. Lack of promise is the major offense at SAB, a school that exists only to mold the promising into full realization of their gifts.

Sexual pressures are intensified in this beautiful and physical world. Everyone is prettier or handsomer than average. Workout clothes are revealing; workouts are sensuous, and partnering means handling and being handled. Kirstein says that dancers are autoerotic; certainly they are exhibitionistic. They must call attention to themselves and the way they move; one hopes they will do so, as Richard Rapp constantly instructs them, ". . . in a good way." That is not always the case. Once, some years ago, an overstimulated female student proceeded to rip off all her clothes and parade around the school naked. She was intercepted, dressed, and sent home to California for a couple of weeks to rest and think. No further punishment was enforced. The tolerance paid off too; Heather Watts is now a famous and thrilling ballerina. "Balanchine had a wonderful understanding of extreme behavior," says Kirstein. "Unless someone is slightly hysterical, it's just not interesting."

To some of the boys, resisting authority, defying the rules, even getting caught and fulfilling the penance while still surviving, can be a badge of honor, a sign of courage and masculinity. To some, being too good, too serious, implies wimpiness, finkiness, femininity. New York City Ballet soloist David Otto has been heard to brag of his SAB days that he was thrown out seven times: "Twice by Mr. Balanchine himself."

SAB does not take on the role of parent or protector to its students, even those who are here alone from far-off cities or lands. Dreamed-of dormitories are still in the planning stages, so housing is up to the individual. There are no guidance counselors at SAB; there is no school nurse. There are no sex-education classes, no lectures pointing out the dangers of needles, pills, peddlers of pot or crack, or of strangers offering candy. There are no sweeps of lockers looking for liquor or drugs, either. SAB's purpose is not to coddle, nurture, or round off rough adolescent edges. Anorexia is expected to be dealt with by parents and/or doctors; plummeting academic grades and scheduling problems are of little interest to the school's staff. Teachers do not feel required to deal with the emotional problems of their students; often they feel strongly that they should stay out of their "normal," non-SAB lives.

SAB exists to churn out beautiful classical dancers. That is its franchise, its only mission. It is a single-minded place with a clear purpose. Kirstein likes to compare it to West Point, another professional academy, just as he favors comparing a life lived in ballet to that of a Jesuit priest. He says, "I was stationed at West Point during the war, and I realized one thing. They are not turning out killers there, and they're not turning out well-rounded diplomats. They're turning out engineers. At SAB we are not interested in turning out beautifully educated, charmingly mannered young men. We are a school for professional dancers!" He adds, "Balanchine was once attacked for not taking the students to museums. He replied, 'I went to a museum once.' "

SAB may seem heartless and cold; in a way it is. It is also, however, a place of amazing purity and shared purpose.

Classical dance is an ideal; SAB teachers are devoted to it. The school can also be a hotbed of competition and comparison, triumph and defeat. It's worse for the girls but intensifying each year for the boys. Rivalries, disagreements, and rows often flare up. The most promising students, the ones with the best ballet bodies and largest potential, are usually gracious and gentle. Down in the pecking order, insecurities and jealousies rear their twisted heads, though, and nastiness itches like a rash. There is bitchiness at SAB, snubbing, occasionally even shouting. But ballet is all about good manners, generosity, chivalry, elegance . . . gentilesse. This is not a Ramboesque world of grunting animals, of solving problems with violence. This is an environment of cooperation, consideration, control. Or at least it's supposed to be.

Now someone—Max—had gone beyond all limits and exploded in class. Never before, never, ever in the more than half a century the school had been in existence had one student hauled off and belted another one—in class! It was as shocking to the SAB hierarchy as it would be to a Jesuit if an armed robbery was staged during High Mass. A ghastly breach of etiquette; but it was even more than that. Without control in ballet, all is lost. Dancers must be able to reach a point of almost complete abandon without ever losing their strong, elastic, in-charge control. Max had lost control, and he had lost it completely, physically. In class. Even Mrs. Gleboff was stunned, and she thought she'd seen just about everything.

When the two Natashas discussed the incident with Krammie and Ms. Finn the morning after, they all came to the one unavoidable conclusion: Max must be banished from the Garden. He must go instantly, and he must never return. The school was humming with gossip and guesswork.

*   *   *

23

Meanwhile, up on Eighty-ninth Street, just west of Broadway, preparing for her foray down to Sixty-sixth and SAB, Brenda Fuqua was conditioning herself to take control of the meeting. If Mrs. Gleboff was permitted to start off on the litany of Max's offenses over the last months, if she got a chance to talk about his skipping so many classes and defiantly breaking the dress code day after day, if she tried to establish the fact that he was rebelling, that he was losing interest and that he was not making the expected progress, all would be lost. Brenda had to cut her off at the pass, never give the director a chance to kick Max out. She dressed carefully, for success, wanting to look calm and competent. She was as nervous as Max, but she had no intention of showing it, to him or anyone else. Swallowing hard and playing her role to the hilt, she ushered Max out of the apartment, down onto Broadway, and into a taxi. Those days, money was a problem and taxis were luxuries, but that day the car was a necessity. No buses; they needed all the moral support they could get.

Purposefully mother and son disembarked in front of the Juilliard building; steadfastly they rode the elevator to the third floor; confidently they strode down the hallway, around the corner, and into Mrs. Gleboff's office. Once in the room, though, in front of the cool clarity of the two Natashas, all efforts at appearing in charge went out the window. Brenda's desires for her son churned right up to the surface. All she could do was talk. So she talked and talked and talked some more. She pleaded and importuned for two hours. Eventually she wore the Russian women down. Max received a two-week suspension, but he would be allowed to come back to the school as soon as he had done his time. Brenda was limp with relief, thrilled at having won. Her world was safe for a while, at least. Commented Mrs. Gleboff, "It really was so shocking.

Max did punch Josh without provocation. The only reason we didn't dismiss him was because his mother begged and begged."

Max said nothing. Without provocation, indeed! The fact that Josh existed was provocation enough for him. The two had been enemies for close to two years now, though once they'd been pretty good chums. Neither one could figure out just exactly what had gone wrong, and each had a completely different story, but both were clear that the friendship was over. Max was more vehement and direct, though, as he proved that fateful day.

III.

One of the Boys

Max and Josh had met in September three years before, the day that Max arrived to take his place at SAB alongside the other teenage male crème de la crème of dance. Josh was already in place. The little Dallasite, Max, was a thirteen-year-old putto. Or so he looked. Short, with plenty of baby fat still clinging to his trunk and limbs, he was blond, large-eyed, and blessed with a pink-and-white complexion and sensuous lips. He was intimidated but doing all he could to appear cocky. He had dressed real Texas-style: A plaid shirt topped his tight, worn jeans, and an Indian belt circled his rather round waist. His stock-in-trade, his feet, were made larger and noisier than life by cowboy boots of lizard skin that had toes pointed so sharp, they could dissect an iguana with one swift kick. He didn't have the courage to go so far as to wear a five-gallon hat (ten would have been too large by far for his small boy's head), but he ambled down the ballet academy's halls as though his noggin were so covered and his right hand were busy swinging a lariat.

Three boys in black tights and white T-shirts were sprawled around the reception area, stretching and gabbing.

They looked up and wondered what on earth was coming toward them. It was four o'clock in the afternoon. "S'cuse me," drawled Max, slow and easy, "but d'y'all know where Intermediate class will be held?" The boys looked up at Max, glanced quizzically at each other, and then, as though well rehearsed, said, "Intermediate? Oh, man, it's over. We finished at four." The three then closed in their little circle and excluded Max. They went on chatting with each other as though he had disappeared, as though they had just corrected the misguided directions of a nomadic delivery boy who had gone on about his business.

"How could it be?" thought Max. "This is my first day. How could I have gotten it wrong?" He had been sure Intermediate was held at five-thirty. What would he do now? His anxiety grew, and his toes started to radiate pain, pinched as they were in reptilian confinement. He made his way to the office, found the secretary, and confirmed that Intermediate Men's class was indeed at five-thirty, in Studio 2. Ah ha. Ignoring his hazers, Max went into the dressing room and found his locker. He released his toes from their imprisonment, donned his tights and T-shirt, and slid his new soft, black ballet slippers on over his throbbing feet. He felt lonely, scared, and totally out of it, but he thought, "I'm gonna have the best class of my life. Today they're all gonna notice Max Fuqua."

Studio 2 was empty, so Max went in and did his stretching there alone, working at the barre, staring at the mirror that filled one whole wall of the room. While lengthening his calves and hamstrings, working them into pliability, he practiced looking cool, blasé, sophisticated. He vowed that no one would see his quaking. Soon the other boys began dribbling in. They were tall and short, thin and plump. They numbered a baker's dozen, and with their braces, pimples, unreliable deep voices, beginning facial stubble, and good-natured shoving, they seemed a glossary of adolescentia. It was hard to believe that this motley crew would turn into Poets of Gesture. They seemed much more like a gaggle of geeks. Bringing up the rear were Max's hazers and Josh. Max pretended not to notice them and set about outshining every-one in the room.

Class began as usual, at the barre, with pliés. Up and down bobbed the boys, knees bending and straightening, first demi-plié, halfway, then grand plié, deep down, fannies almost touching the floor. Learning how to bend the knees properly, easily and with good balance, is one of the most vital exercises for young dancers. Nothing in ballet is possible without proper pliés; exercises always start with them. Then tendus, ronds de jambe, etc., etc., etc., logically building up strength, balance, flexibility, turnout, laying the foundation for the combination of steps to follow. Richard Rapp was teaching class today. The logic of what and how he teaches is clearer, more visible than that of any other teacher. His class builds upon itself constantly, ever increasing in size, speed, and complexity. To Max the ninety-minute session was end-less, excruciating, confusing, more difficult even for his mind than his body. He was really working full out, trying to show the others in his class they had someone to deal with. It was agony.

Says Richard Rapp, "You know, when I was with the City Ballet, Balanchine always used to say, 'Boys are lazy.' And he was right. We had it easy. There were few enough of us that the competition was nothing like what it was with the girls. That has changed now, but the boys are still lazy. They need to be awakened, startled. When Balanchine taught

Barre exercises and the omnipresent mirror.

company class, he would give us the most impossible, mind-numbing combinations, and we would gaze at him, dumb-founded. He would look back and say, calmly, 'Try and do, boys. Is good for the brain.' "

Says Josh about Mr. Rapp, "He gets a big kick out of confusing people. Then he'll say, 'A*wwwww*l right. I think we can simplify this a bit more.' I'll never forget one time, when I was in A-2 (the level before Intermediate), we were taking class at the State Theater. Someone screwed up. Mr. Rapp looked at the kid, shook his head, shrugged his shoulders, and said, 'There's always college.' "

Class went on. Rapp gave Max some corrections, and Max tried to incorporate them. The eyes of Texas were no longer on the boy, but he was being sized up by every student in the room—and also by the teacher. He tried very hard to do what was being asked of him, but he simply couldn't manage to do it all, to make all the changes he was being instructed to make. He started to get mad. "Everyone has always said I was such a good dancer," he thought. "Why is everything I do suddenly so wrong?" Then he looked around the room, checked out the competition. Fear joined fury. There were so many other boys. Some were at least as good as he was; some were better. Most non-dancers don't have to come to grips with such heavy competition until college. Max was being hit with it just as he was trying to get used to being a teenager.

His brain ached. So did his legs, thighs, hips, shoulders, arms, and neck. Not to mention his heart. All his life Max had been special, prized. He was the only one to be a ballet dancer in his family, and the only boy who danced in his class, his neighborhood, his whole school. He was unique, and everyone told him so, especially his mother. Max was his mother's favorite, and she was thrilled that he was a dancer. Now there were all these others. Would that make Max less special to his mom? Would she favor him less now? Brenda Fuqua had been dying to be associated with the arts, and Max was her passport. He knew that and liked it; he liked the status it gave him in the family, and he didn't want to change. Nonconforming was a prized Fuqua characteristic, and Brenda felt that the arts offered safe haven for nonconformists. Says she, "I have always tried to have my children look and dress like everyone else, and I have always tried my damnedest to have them not *be* like everyone else."

Highland Park, the suburb of Dallas where Max lived until he moved to New York, was established, moneyed, traditional. Max's family was untraditional, unmoneyed, not interested in being established. His father, who himself grew up in Highland Park, is a geologist who also owns a health-food store. Stephen Fuqua doesn't think that ballet is a worthwhile endeavor for a boy—he thinks ballet is "fluff"—and he wishes Max were preparing himself better to earn a living. It's an extremely common argument against ballet for boys, particularly boys from traditional backgrounds. Max's father is anything but traditional, however. He is, according to his son, "kind of a rebel in our town." As a geologist, he searches for oil or precious minerals; he thinks he and his partners are now coming up with some in Arizona. As the owner of a health-food store, he regularly takes on the medical establishment, feeling that they are "failing us with sixty-five diseases." Says Max, "What I like best about my dad is

Max is the only boy in his Dallas class.

that he's not really rich, and he doesn't have many women friends, but he's happy. He doesn't plan things; he thinks plans get in the way. One minute he'll be in the store, and the next he'll go to this farm he has in northeast Texas. With Dad religion is important; he gets guidance from it and things like that. Clothes are no big deal to him. He doesn't own a real suit."

What Max likes best about his mother, he says, is her I-don't-give-a-damn attitude. "If she doesn't want to explain something to someone, she doesn't," says her son. Brenda Fuqua was born and raised in Beaufort, Louisiana, and says her family was "extremely traditional." Her mother was adventurous, though, says Brenda; she was "the first to bob her hair or drive a car." She died in childbirth when Brenda was just five and a half years old. Brenda doesn't remember grieving terribly as a child, though she does remember "being a brat," and she says she now misses her mother more than ever. Max says that he and his mother are both romantics. "We both like things to be soft and beautiful." He pauses and then adds, "I was always a mama's boy. The other kids in the family made up a song that they used to sing to me all the time: 'He's b*iiiiiii*g Max. He's ru*ffff*; he's tu*fffff*; he's m*eeeee*an, and' "—sotto voce—" 'he loves his mommy.' I don't know," muses the son, "I'll probably be living with my mother when I'm sixty."

Max's mother and father were married just ten days after they met, and they were divorced ten years after they were married. Their parting was extremely acrimonious; Max's father is still furious with his mother, and the two speak only when it is absolutely necessary. Brenda has six children; three are Fuquas and three are Mullens, the name of her husband before Max's father. Stephen Fuqua (called Etienne by his mother) is older than Max, and Brenda is younger. The

three Mullens are Lana, Louis, and Alice. Each child is very
different from all the others. Louis, Max's oldest brother, was
a fine gymnast in high school; he actually brought the sport to
his school. Now in his early twenties, Louis is studying
filmmaking at the University of New Mexico in Albuquerque.
He is a serious Christian who thinks that Woody Allen is a
good filmmaker but really "a fool." Says Max about Louis,
"He wasn't real popular in school, but everybody knew who
he was." Says his mother, "The spring before Louis was to
graduate, he was half a credit short, and the school was being
very sticky about it. Then one day at the lunch break Louis
did a handstand on the roof of the school building. Somehow
they managed to find the half credit and get him out of there."
Max's oldest sister, Lana, was the painter of the family, Alice
the musician, and so it went.

Max was the dancer. If that meant he had to take some
crap from kids at school and from the occasional sadistic
football coach, so be it. It almost made him feel good. The
last thing in the world he wanted was to be a real part of
Highland Park life, and at ballet school he was considered
almost a national treasure. He was adorable to look at, able to
do anything they asked, and blessed with a sense of humor.
He was *it*—teacher's pet, Mommy's pet, a little darling. All
the baby ballerinas had crushes on him, and most of his
friends regarded him with a real measure of envy. He starred
in every single production the school put on, and one Christmas he even had to take six roles in the annual pageant. He
bitched about it at home, complained about how much work
it all was, but he loved it, loved being so singled out, loved all
the attention. Being a dancer gave Max approval and love
everywhere he turned, as well as an exotic appeal. He was
very successful at being different.

And now, here he was, one of many, not different, not

the only and not the best, with a teacher who had no attachment to him at all—in a city where he knew no one. Suddenly Max felt as though he were nothing, that everyone else was better, ahead of him. He hated it; it was humiliating—and frightening. How *would* his mother react?

Somehow he lived through that first class, and when it was over, he bravely gave his three joke-playing classmates a big smile to show that he was a good sport, that he was no

Just before making the big leap to New York.

goody-two-slippers, and that he wasn't as afraid as he really was. All his life Max had practiced hiding his emotions, his fears, his confusion. All through his parents' endless fights and eventual divorce he mastered the art of seeming untroubled, and he planned to get even better at it. No one would know how tiny he felt today. No one would ever know.

The other boys responded to his seeming carefreeness, and soon Max was accepted as one of them. Mark became his closest friend, but Josh was a pal as well. Mark is a New Yorker, born and bred, a freckle-faced carrot-top who hails from a long line of redheaded athletes. He started ballet lessons to aid his hockey playing, but it was soon apparent that he had exceptional dance ability, and hockey was put aside. At fourteen, Mark was in the Special Men's class at SAB. He had been invited at thirteen, but his academic schedule couldn't permit extra dance time. Mark was the youngest boy in Special, and the one dancer from Intermediate to be so honored.

Special Men's class, which was started by Balanchine in 1982, is an additional class daily for the most elite of the elite, a chance for the especially prized to get additional instruction in a highly concentrated small group. It's like honors algebra, only better. A handful of these stars of tomorrow are selected by Stanley and Krammie and permitted to add Special to their schedules and their personas. In a world with a hierarchy that would make the Indian caste system pale by comparison, the Special Men's students are the Brahmans of the Brahmans. Every ballet student, male or female, and every ballet dancer constantly lives to be the chosen one. Dancers walk an emotional tightrope all the time. The balance can be tipped so easily—by an injury, a death in the family, even a large meal. Dancers' lives are fueled by

35

uncertainty and anxiety. "Will I be noticed?" is always on the dancer's mind. "Will I be selected for the class/company/role/ promotion? Am I special?" Dancers work and work and work to try to achieve the unachievable, and then they must wait for someone else to give the nod. They are never in control of their futures, and they are always the instruments of someone else's control. Ambition they must have in large doses, but pursuing a part or a job the way a business executive can pursue an account doesn't work. Politics runs rampant in ballet schools and companies—probably slightly more than in huge universities and corporations and slightly less than in the Catholic Church—but politics without special ability, looks, and interpretation won't do anyone any good. Ballet dancers hunger for recognition. *Special* is a key word in their lexicon.

Mark was being recognized; he was one of the Special Men. He managed always to be self-effacing with his pals; he never lorded it over them; and he took a lot of teasing about being Special from his envious classmates. Privately, of course, he was thrilled—why not?—and he worked very hard to prove himself worthy of the privilege.

Mark and Max often went to Central Park together that fall, sometimes with other boys, including Josh, to play touch football or throw Frisbees. Sometimes they combined both and played an invented game that used a Frisbee as a replacement for a football. When the SAB boys play touch football, it's always just a little different from the game the Trinity or Collegiate or St. David's or P.S. 103 boys play. It's faster, for one, and more graceful for two. Pirouettes and grand battements are used to dodge opponents. A tour-en-l'air pass draws approving murmurs, and a jeté over the goal line is greeted with applause from teammates and opponents alike. The winners always take extravagant bows, too. These are dancers, after all.

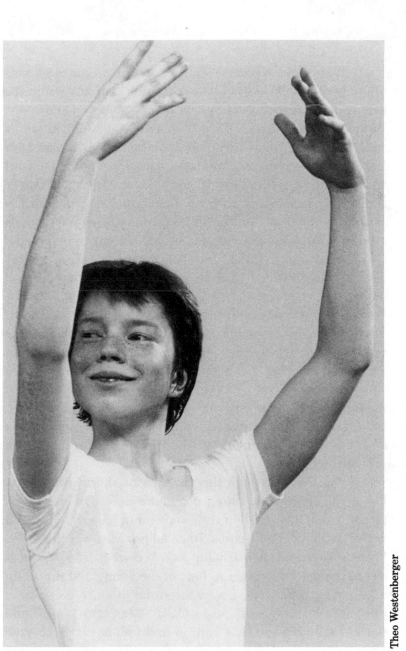

Max's friend Mark, in Special Men's class.

Sometimes Max and Mark went without the other kids to the park to talk, or ride bikes, or smoke, or just watch the goings-on, and there was always plenty going on. For New Yorkers, Central Park is a big backyard; it is where city kids and city adults go to play. No suburban pool, cookout, or Little League game ever offered a fraction of the delights of Mr. Olmsted's green oasis in the middle of Manhattan. In addition to restaurants, concerts, free performances of Shakespeare, a carousel, and a bird sanctuary, the park boasts dozens of roller skaters and skateboarders competing on soda-can-marked slalom runs, and ball games of every variety played side by side, with an occasional errant soccer ball inhibiting the progress to first base of a softball heavy hitter. Pockets of folk dancing celebrate varied ethnic backgrounds; martial arts classes practice bowing formally before hurling each other to the ground; and actors regularly enact bogus duels to the death. Singers trill; musicians practice scales alfresco; and on the park road, bikers, joggers, and race walkers all compete for lanes. There are horses and dogs, beautiful girls, schmoozers, cruisers, and bruisers, plus a distinctly urban bird of prey who can quickly sniff out the unsuspecting.

Max had met with this last species shortly after arriving in the city. While riding their bikes one day he and his brother Stephen joined up with some other teenage riders and set off to discover new paths for pedaling. Max was thrilled to know some non-ballet-dancing kids; he went back the next day to ride with them again. One of the younger of the group asked if he could try Max's special dirt bike, a going-away present from his best friend in Dallas. Max said "Sure," and the kid rode off—and off and off and off, never to be seen again. It's an old Central Park ploy, but the Texan was

38

dumbfounded, then furious. He and his mother vowed to catch the culprit.

First Max rode around in a police car, looking for the boy and/or the bike. No luck. A couple of weeks later, though, he saw the lad in a group. He called the police, then his mother. She rushed to the park and devised a stalling tactic. Playacting a distraught mother, she rolled her eyes and quaveringly wailed, "*Ohhhhhhhhhh*, *noooo*, won't someone please help me. Won't someone help me find my little girl. I'll give ten dollars to anyone who'll help me find my baby."

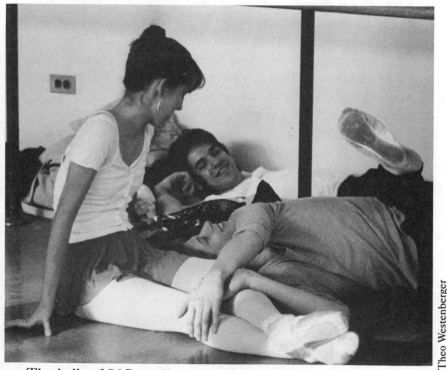

The halls of SAB are littered with boys and bunheads.

Theo Westenberger

39

Max's suspect approached Brenda and told her she should be more careful, that Central Park could be a dangerous place for a little girl. She delayed the boy just long enough for the police to arrive, handcuff him, and take him to the station house. Brenda went along and filled out a complaint; she later dropped charges when the boy's parents offered to pay for the bike. She says, "I'm a big believer in law and order. Criminals should pay for their crimes, no matter how old they are." The boy was eleven.

Sometimes Max would go over to Mark's house after school; other times he'd go home with Josh. He didn't like bringing his new friends to his own apartment. His mother would be there; she would tell them what to do and butt into their conversations. They couldn't be themselves. When he went over to Josh's, the two would watch television or talk about how tough Mr. Rapp was or gossip about the bunheads at the school. Bunheads, of course, are the girls, the budding ballerinas with the topknots. In ballet dancer's colloquial, though, bunheads are also those who are only interested in ballet, who are obsessed with classical dance. Most of the girls are bunheads, seriously committed to ballet. Each of them is prettier than the next, and the boys never tire of thinking or talking about them. What they can't understand, though, is why these gorgeous girls are so obsessed with just ballet and food, how they can talk and talk and talk about what they did eat, didn't eat, would eat, could eat, and wanted to eat, or about class or a performance they had seen, or about ballet gossip they had heard. The boys would get sick of talking about it—or listening to it. "Bunheads!" they would gripe, bewildered.

IV.

Nuts

J osh is so good-looking, he is almost as pretty as a bunhead. Brown wavy hair frames his heart-shaped face, and huge brown eyes peer out from it. He's an only child; his mother was a dancer; his father is in advertising. Like Max, Josh's parents moved with him to New York. Unlike Max, his parents are together; together they changed their lives for their son. Says Mrs. Gleboff, "You know, all the parents say they never put pressure on their children, but moving here for them . . ." Her voice trails off; her shoulders shrug slightly.

It's a tough decision for a family. Being accepted at SAB is a major opportunity for a young dancer, and the school has no housing for its students. Some of the dancers board with families; others live at Y's; still others share apartments without any adult supervision. How many parents would feel confident sending their twelve- or thirteen-year-old to live with strangers or on their own in a huge city like New York? What do they do? What are their options? Do they split up the family, with Mom coming to New York for the sake of her talented Terpsichorean, leaving Dad and the other less privileged kids in Dubuque or Des Moines? The answer is often

41

yes. We all know what happened in *The Turning Point*, though, don't we? The temptations for child and mother were all there and were very tempting indeed. Many nuclear families would burst apart under such pressure, and lots of folks are not willing to take the risk.

"Every year," says Lincoln Kirstein, "we miss out on some very talented dancers because we cannot house them. They are accepted and they just don't show up." Kirstein is spearheading, with his brains, his connections, and a pledge of $1 million of his own money, a campaign to get dormitories built for SAB students. Meanwhile family sacrifices will continue to be made in the cause of perpetuating this precious and fragile art form, ballet. For Josh's parents there was no sacrifice in leaving Ohio. One visit back to Dayton made them vow never again to leave the isle of Manhattan. For Max's mother, his acceptance at SAB meant a real chance. "Let's say coming for Max was the socially acceptable way for me to leave Dallas and move to New York," she says.

Brenda Fuqua, the daughter, was not pleased at all when she learned she would be leaving her friends and school in Texas and moving to the Big Apple just for the sake of the Big Brother. The youngest Fuqua could live without her brother Max entirely; she is tired of his feeling free to take her tapes, her clothes, and anything else he thinks he might use, and she is particularly tired of having to live her life around his, of his getting everything he wants and getting away with murder too. She's also tired of being the youngest. However, she was but ten at coming-East time, with no other option but to obey her mother, so move she did. She has adjusted. She doesn't mind New York anymore, but she dislikes her yucky brother more and more every day.

The Fuquas' first New York Christmas, Max had a part

in the City Ballet's *Nutcracker*—just a small one, as one of the young guests in the opening party scene, but it was still a part. Every year some ninety children from SAB are selected to perform in the company's holiday classic. They are chosen for poise and ability—and also for size. The younger children are the desired ones, and they must correctly fit the existing costumes; it's just too expensive any other way. Still, it's a real sign of status to be selected; to be the correct age and size and left out is to be exiled to Siberia. Max was thrilled. He hadn't been at SAB very long; already he was with the "ins." He had been selected for a part, and that's the best kind of chosen. Performing is the lifeblood of even very young student dancers. Being onstage is the reward; it's what makes all the long, horrible hours in the classroom worthwhile. *The Nutcracker* is the kids' yearly chance to get up there and show 'em, especially the boys. There are more parts in *The Nutcracker* for boys than there are for girls, and many an American lad has been talked into staying with his tedious ballet lessons only by the promise of a juicy part at Christmastime. Max wasn't one of those; his reasons for staying with his lessons were different, but still he loves performing, loves applause, loves being loved by an audience. And he loved being in *The Nutcracker.* He rarely loves class.

Ballet class is a world in miniature, where every little movement really does have a meaning all its own. Coaxing young bodies into the correct turnout, mastering the proper arm and head positions, honing ronds de jambe and ports de bras are the mission, the components of dance class. Repetition is the method. At the barre, day after day, over and over. It's very hard for young boys to stay interested, not to get bored or frustrated, or both. Even the end-of-class leaps and spins don't always relieve the tension that builds with such focused concentration on the minuscule. Boys study dance in class, and they study hard.

Onstage they dance. They work hard, too, but the difference is like night and day. Performing doesn't sap energy; it provides it, and also gives a real purpose to all those excruciating hours. Onstage there is excitement; there are costumes; there is makeup, and, most important, there is that sea of happy faces out there. Says a sage eight-year-old from Washington, D.C., "I like *Nutcracker* because I'm in the merry scenes. What I like to do is go out there and make people in the audience happy."

For over a dozen years David Richardson was in charge of the children for the New York City Ballet's *Nutcracker*. Richardson chose the students at auditions, taught them their parts, and rehearsed them. As a youngster, he had been in the production himself, as the little prince; his understanding of *Nutcracker*'s importance to the kids is complete. "Being onstage is what makes you want to continue," says Richardson. "It gives you a taste of what you might be able to get in your life."

The Nutcracker may give boys purpose, inspiration, and a chance for ego-fulfillment, but the ballet does even more than that, much more. In America its job is threefold. First, *Nutcracker* acts as a siren's song, singing the pleasures of classical dance, each year bringing countless innocents under its spell. Most Americans are introduced to ballet by *Nuts*, as the dancers call the *Nutcracker*. They see it as small children, at holiday time, with their whole families; and chances are that an older brother or sister will be up on the stage, having the time of his/her life and inspiring the younger kids to do the same.

Nutcracker is a perfect ballet for one's first. It is an

easily accessible fairy tale, a mystery in which good soundly triumphs over evil. It is also available to short attention spans, and at least some of the music has been heard by even the smallest children before they ever see the ballet, so their ears help their eyes "get" what is going on. Add the fact that the stage is usually filled with their own kind, and you can understand why *Nutcracker* is such a hit with children. Comments David Richardson, "I think, country-wide, the reason *Nutcracker* is so effective in bringing new generations into classical dance is that their first experience with the ballet is generally such a pleasant one, and that it is so rooted in a warm experience with the family."

Nutcracker is fun; fun that glorifies classical dance. Boys who see *Nuts* once and boys who dance in it every year all get the same message. This is a good time. Ballet dancing becomes a good thing for boys to do, especially if it means being in *Nutcracker*. Says Richardson, "*Nutcracker* is the one ballet that the children's contemporaries in regular school have all heard of. So it's obvious that it is very prestigious for them to appear in it. I won't exactly compare it to the Olympics, but if you are doing something outside of school, and that something is dance, *Nutcracker* is the one ballet that the others know about and have respect for. The boys are never afraid to tell their friends that they are in *Nutcracker*."

Before it was acceptable on these shores for boys to take ballet lessons, most of the *Nutcracker* parts, for both boys and girls, were filled by girls. That has changed—everywhere. It was in 1977 that the New York City Ballet finally was able to put together a full regiment of *real* boy soldiers, and the difference they make to the production is profound.

The boys in *Nutcracker* must move with grace and elegance, but the grace is a masculine, courtly one, which finds its opposite in the delicate, feminine movements for the girls. Though young boys are often shy at first about "relating" to the girls in *Nutcracker*'s opening party scene, they soon become accustomed to their partners, and after a while they even enjoy showing off their menacing swordplay to delighted gasps and high-pitched giggles.

Says Richardson, recalling Christmases past, "When the party scene was all girls, and girls dressed up as boys, the interplay didn't have the bite it took on when real boys started taking the parts." He continues, "Often, at the start of rehearsals, the boys and girls don't want to touch each other. If it were just a school performance or a recital, they might rebel and not go through with it. But this is *Nutcracker*, and

His father helps a *Nutcracker* prince into his costume.

The prince onstage.

they are all told, 'You *have* to take the girl by the waist; you *have* to hold her arm.' By the time they have worked on it for a while and have been groomed some more, they really start to enjoy that sensation of being elegant and showing off the girls. They also enjoy showing off *for* the girls, and the girls like it too. It was just too relaxed when the girls played the boys' parts. There was no true tension between them, and it was obvious to the audience too. That chemistry makes for a better look on the stage. The whole party scene became clarified better when the boys joined."

Perhaps the most magical moment in the NYCB *Nutcracker* takes place when the tree sprouts up from the floor and grows and grows until it takes over the stage. Children watching squeal, and adults catch their breath in delighted disbelief. Balanchine himself used to say, "The tree is the ballet." Around the base of this enormous evergreen, dancers dressed as soldiers and mice stage their battle, cheered on by little party-goers. It's a comic war of swords and shoves, but every year during the chaos of combat, unscheduled casualties occur. Soldiers slip and fall, and mice crash into each other. Youngsters also tumble down through the trapdoor that releases the tree. During Max's first *Nutcracker* in New York, a soldier friend of his was watching his little mouse girlfriend scurry about when suddenly she disappeared—*poof!*—literally down the hatch. She wasn't hurt, and he managed somehow not to fall apart right on the stage, thereby learning an important performing skill, one that could never be taught in class. In other productions around the country, thrones have tipped over and dumped their princes and princesses unceremoniously into the footlights; mouse kings have lost their elaborate crowns and been reduced to panicked kids; curtains have closed and left tiny angels abandoned onstage, in front of the velvet, without a clue as to how to get off. All this can happen to adults too. Ballerinas and danseurs alike must learn to pick themselves up after a fall and get right back in step on the right beat. Costumes rip; snow machines refuse to stop, turning stages into slippery fog banks; scrims collapse. Performing in *Nutcracker* starts a young dancer off on the road to a calm confidence that will allow him to deal professionally with the mini-disasters that will become a part of his onstage life.

In addition to learning not to panic, that they are always visible if they are onstage, and that they must behave accordingly, even if the action is elsewhere, *Nutcracker* children learn to project themselves, and they get practice in conquering stage fright and developing presence. They get a sense of the importance of timing, and they learn how to correctly pantomime a response so that the audience can read what it is they are communicating with their bodies. None of these performance skills can be learned in the classroom. They need the urgency of necessity to be mastered properly. It also takes going to rehearsals—having a *real* rehearsal to go to—to learn how important it is to be on time with your costume on properly—and to be quiet while waiting for cues.

Says Richardson, "During rehearsals for *Nutcracker*, the children learn that dancing is much, much more than tendu and plié. It's an extension of yourself, and when you're on the stage, you are not necessarily only giving the steps. You're giving your person to the audience and the way you present the steps. You are so naked when you are on the stage. Children wouldn't realize this; even some adult dancers don't realize it. To give this quality you need coaching. You need someone to help you. You need to trust, and you have to understand that it's necessary."

He continues, "The children are all individuals; they

49

all bring their own selves to their parts. Some of the little bits of business in *Nutcracker*, especially with the lead parts, were not choreographed; they were put there by children. A child would do a little business, a certain way of waking up, perhaps, and I'd like it and keep it in for the next year. I may have been the one in charge during rehearsals, but it was and always will be theirs on the stage." Says Max, "What you really learn from being in *Nutcracker* is that you can't just do the steps they teach you in class."

Boys like Max, who are lucky enough or talented enough, or both, to be in the production of a major company, can also find themselves side by side with the top men in their profession, with their role models. Where else does this happen? Not at Harvard, not at IBM, not in the military, not even in the Society of Jesus.

Max's first Christmas Peter Martins danced the part of the Cavalier many times. The Danish dancer, who is now the cochairman of the SAB faculty, was the little Texan's hero, idol, and demigod. Suddenly there they were, onstage together, and Martins would chat with him during rehearsals. Sometimes Martins even said hello first. Take that, Highland Park. Max was enthralled, and he was bowled over to see how hard his hero worked. He saw the star rehearse again and again and again a role he had been performing for many years, and he also saw him at the barre, practicing his tendus and pliés just like every other ballet dancer in the world. Seeing one's idol make such an effort, sweating, hurting, and trying again and again is a lesson that can only be absorbed in person. No one could ever have told Max what tremendous work and concentration went into a Martins performance. He would have said, "Oh, yeah, sure." Performing with the Great Dane, though, Max saw for himself the meaning of the word *professional.* The lesson, heavy with impact, was etched indelibly on his psyche.

For the young Dallasite, a major side benefit of being in *Nutcracker* that first year was snow. His first snow. During rehearsal breaks he and his new friends would rush out to the Lincoln Center promenade and roll around in the stuff and have snowball fights and smear the white iciness in each other's faces. Max's mother wouldn't have approved of all this, but she didn't even have to know about it. Rehearsals belonged to Max, and he guarded every minute of them jealously. He didn't want to share them with anyone, even her. She came to all the performances, of course, but that was okay, especially since she was mostly out front and not backstage, and even more especially because she was so pleased with her son. Says Brenda of her boy, "I just love to watch him onstage. I know that I can't be great myself, but I also know that I can be Max's mother."

There is a progression in *Nuts,* just as there is in every other aspect of ballet. Party scene or mouse or soldier or hoops or tea or younger brother or cavalier; each part is for a certain age and a certain skill level. Danseurs can, and often do, spend their entire careers in the work. George Balanchine, for example, was twelve when he was first in *Nuts* at St. Petersburg's Maryinsky Theater, and seventy-five when he last played Herr Drosslemeyer in his own version for American television. Jacques d'Amboise started right at the top in the NYCB *Nutcracker,* as the Cavalier, and he danced the role enough years to be joined on the stage by his own son, Christopher. Peter Martins grew up in the Royal Danish Ballet's version of *Nutcracker* and made his American debut as the Cavalier with the New York City Ballet. When he retired from the stage in 1983 to take over for the then ailing

Balanchine, Martins donned his white tights one last time and danced a farewell performance of the beloved role that left hardly a dry eye in the house.

Nutcracker is the most popular ballet in the world, the whole world. The U.S. has become the Russian-born ballet's true home, however, and each year many thousands of Americans watch snowflakes fly, flowers waltz, and a wooden toy turn into a handsome prince. Every Christmas 102,600 children and adults see the New York City Ballet production, and that's just one of the hundreds of versions of *Nuts* to be seen live, on television, or now even at the movie theater. *Nutcracker* recruits and teaches, and it also makes enough money to keep companies and schools—indeed, classical dance itself—alive on these shores. The manager of a small company out West has said, "We have a fall season, a spring season, and a *Nutcracker* season. The *Nutcracker* season pays the bills."

For Max's second New York *Nutcracker* he was selected for a bigger part than the first year. He was to do the Candy Cane Dance—or Hoops, as the kids call it. This time he would don a candy-striped costume and get out there and do some real dancing—with a big, round hoop. It's a favorite role for the kids, and Max couldn't wait for his chance. His friend Chris was originally supposed to dance Hoops, but Max was put in instead. Chris felt rejected and insulted to be replaced without explanation. The new kid had swiped his part, and Chris was learning very young about how fragile a dancer's grasp is on what he views as his own. He snarled at Max and said, "Oh, why don't you go back where you came from." Max just smiled. He was feeling smug and triumphant; he reveled in winning, in beating out Chris, in getting a meaty part. SAB classrooms are filled with huge and hungering egos. Each and every boy in Intermediate was used to being a pet.

Now each had to learn to be one of many, all of whom were vying for a spot as teacher's pet, someone's pet, everyone's pet. Chris and Max had been pitted against each other; only one would win. This time it was Max's turn, but Chris would get his chance. Few know instinctively what these boys will someday realize: that comparisons are destructive and that they must learn to compete only with themselves. Just then, though, they were too young and too insecure for such insight.

So here was Chris, dejected and seething, and here was Max, envisioning himself as stealing the whole *Nutcracker* show from Peter Martins. Max planned to dazzle the audiences at the State Theater, impress his friends and teachers, and wow his mother. She would be brimming with pride. He couldn't wait to call Texas, either, to speak to his former teacher. He could just imagine himself casually dropping the news: "Oh, yes, I'll be in Nutcracker again this year. No, no, not just the party scene this time, although we all have to be in that. No. This year I'll be doing Hoops. You know, Candy Cane." The response, as he planned it, would include a quick intake of breath—"Hoops?"—then an impressed sigh—"W*eeeeelllll*"—followed by an adoring "Of course. Of course . . .. it was just a matter of time. We always knew you would make it big."

V.

Too Young

This year, rehearsals were less fun for Max than last. He had to work harder, and some of his former friends, like Chris, were no longer so close. "Their loss," he would think cavalierly to himself. Now he was getting in with Andrew and those boys; they were the ones he really wanted as friends. They were a couple of years older than Max; Andrew was sixteen, and he already had his own apartment. He was even handsomer than most of the boys and was a big hit with the girls too. And was he ever wild. Peerless. There was nothing Drew wouldn't do, it seemed, and he was letting Max into his inner circle. Josh tagged along, but he was never invited the way Max was. Who needed those other kids? Max had hit the big time.

It just might be that the ancient Greeks were right. Maybe pride—the kind they called *hubris*—is the major sin; maybe a little arrogance is a great affront to the gods. Who knows? That December, though, Max's troubles began. So did his hatred for Josh. As Max tells the story, one day at a *Nuts* rehearsal he and Josh were kidding around, poking each other, jabbing a bit, wrestling some. Suddenly, Max says, Josh got serious about it and started to really punch. Alarmed,

Max broke away from Josh's viselike hold, told him that he thought he was a psycho, and stopped the friendship right then and there. "After that," says Max, "whenever Josh was around, there was this feeling of . . . *bam!*"

That's Max's story. Josh has a different tale. He says he can't really pinpoint the exact beginning of their enmity but that Max sure "started acting like the kids at PCS." Those were the kids that Josh couldn't stand, the students he went to academic classes with at the private Professional Children's School. PCS kids think they are special; basically they are. They are all actors and singers and dancers. The school charges hefty tuition fees to make high school possible for kids with hefty other demands on their time. Classes are tiny, and individual attention is always available, plus they can take courses by correspondence if scheduling ever becomes a problem. Josh, who was used to *A*'s and *B*'s, got bad grades at PCS. One of his teachers called him an "enigma." He says of himself that he was "widely known but not much liked" there. Many SAB kids go to PCS, and the schools are equally competitive. If other prep-school students impress each other with tales of trips to Bermuda or the Alps for holidays, with notices of early acceptance at Harvard or Yale, PCS'ers vie with each other with talk of parts in movies, commercial residuals, of agents competing for their signatures. Academic cares are hardly uppermost in their minds. NYCB star Sean Lavery graduated from PCS and says, "It's a wonder I can spell."

Most of the boys who are in Advanced Men's and Special Men's at SAB go to PCS—if they go to school at all, as their dance classes take up three hours of each morning, not including stretching, showering, dressing, and undressing. Most other schools can't and/or won't accommodate such regular absences. Josh wasn't yet in Advanced, but he was at PCS, anyhow. And now he saw in Max all that he disliked in those snotty, smug kids. That wasn't the whole story, though. That wasn't all that bothered him about Max.

There was an incident that Josh would never forget. It had happened just before *Nutcracker* that year. Josh and Chris and yet another Chris were in the SAB dressing room one day after class when Max came in and found his clothes missing. He thought the three boys had hidden his things, but they said they hadn't. His good blazer worried Max the most. It was very expensive and it was gone; his mother would really give it to him when she found out. The three swore they hadn't touched anything of Max's. He didn't believe them, but after scouring every corner of the dressing room without finding his stuff, Max went home. When he told his mother about what had happened, she flew into a rage. She was sure one of the three boys had Max's things, and she was determined to prove it. Dragging her son along with her, Brenda stormed the homes of the two Chrises and demanded to search their rooms and closets. She went through everything they owned, but she never turned up Max's clothes. She also never went to Josh's home; her son was so humiliated, she finally gave in to his pain, and the two went home. Now Max says Brenda suffered from "a classic case of overreaction."

While Josh was muddling through his days at PCS, Max was bouncing from school to school. The first year he was in New York he and his brother went to the Mt. Pleasant Christian Academy, a Baptist school. It was like going to a one-room schoolhouse on the Upper West Side of Manhattan. Every day the handful of students were given assignments and put into a room to complete them. There was no instruction; there were no lectures, no lab experiments, no slides, nothing to grab the wandering attention or help ignite a spark of interest in a subject. Teachers would check the work done and be available to answer a few questions, but the students were really on their own. It was hard and it was lonely. Max made no friends at that school. It wasn't just that they were all black except for him and his brother; it wasn't just that he was a dancer or a Texan or a non-city kid, either. It was all these things and more, but Mt. Pleasant certainly wasn't the place for him.

The next year Max transferred to LaSalle Academy, a Jesuit-run school on the Lower East Side. That's what he needed his blazer for; LaSalle is a school with a dress code. His mother thought that the Catholic school would be firm in the discipline department, and she was more than right. Max hated it. He thought they were nit-picking, that they were much more interested in their rules than in him. That's what SAB specialized in, too, he thought, insistence on the minus-cule. The kids at LaSalle never accepted Max; they called him Maxi-Pad and made fun of the fact that he was a dancer.

Max really tried at LaSalle, tried to be accepted by students and teachers alike, but it never worked. He even went out for sports, determined that he would make it to the track team. The tryout consisted of a timed run up Second Avenue, from Fourth to Fourteenth Streets and back again. The distance was a mile; to make the team the boys had to run it in less than ten minutes. There was tremendous traffic, under motor and on foot, and every corner had a traffic light. There was also one kid who ran like a whippet. He was the best, and he was the one Max wanted to beat. For two weeks Max prepared; he gulped down loads of vitamins and slept extra hours. The day arrived, and the starting gun went off. Max tore up Second Avenue, dodging potholes and pedestrians, almost exploding his lungs with the effort. He turned around at Fourteenth and rushed back to the school. It worked. He had done it. He had run the mile in six minutes, beaten the star, and made the team. At last, he thought, he would have something that would make the other kids look up to him, make them realize that he was somebody special.

Max hadn't counted on one thing, though. When he got to his five-thirty ballet class that day, he could hardly move. Muscles he hadn't thought about since he was eight knotted up and screamed out in pain. His leg cramps had leg cramps. Running with the track team would ruin his ballet; he couldn't do both. Running would have to go, would have to go the way baseball and football and gymnastics had before it. Max had been a promising athlete. He had started dance because his gymnastics coach thought he should. Then ballet made him give up sports. Ballet had insisted that he give up anything else that competed with her; she demanded all his time and attention, and he was getting fed up with her. Ever since the age of seven he had been regularly relinquishing "normal" pursuits, and he was beginning to wonder whether it was worth it. Being in *Nutcracker* was great . . . but all the other stuff? And all the other boys; they were all so good, and they were mostly taller than he was. He was constantly getting corrections from Mr. Rapp, and it was great to have the attention, but couldn't he do anything right? Wasn't he ever good enough?

The second semester that year, Max transferred to Power Memorial Academy, another Catholic high school . . . bigger this time, nearer SAB, and much cheaper. Money had become very tight in the Fuqua family. Max's mother was just starting a job in real estate and not earning much; his father often didn't send the child support, and there were the other kids as well.

The profit from the sale of their Dallas home was basically what they were living on, and the amount was dwindling rapidly, especially since they had bought their crummy apartment. None of them much liked their new home, but it was supposed to be a good investment; the plan was that it would make them some money just like their house in Dallas had. In the meantime, though, snazzy blazers were out for Max, as were expensive schools. At least for now. His mother intended to make it big one day, but for the present it was Power Memorial.

"Oh, well," Max thought, "at least Stephen and I have the best and biggest room in the apartment." At least they were out of Highland Park, and in fact, he didn't really mind Power. In fact, he kind of liked being around all the tall black jocks. Power drew basketball players the way SAB drew dancers. The mere mention of graduate Lew Alcindor—Kareem Abdul Jabbar now—sent Power students into dreams of picks, rolls, and huge salaries in much the same way that the name Mikhail Baryshnikov sent SAB'ers into fantasies about perfect multiple pirouettes and cries of "Bravo." Neither group was in this for chemistry or Latin or home ec. Academic school for dancers is usually an afterthought, something they simply have to get out of the way.

Says Mrs. Gleboff, "By the level they reach at fifteen or sixteen, when it begins to count, they can't realistically go to demanding academic schools." There are exceptions, of course. Michael Byars, an SAB graduate now dancing beautifully with the NYCB, graduated from the rigorous Stuyvesant High School, a city public school that specializes in science, screens top students with tough entrance exams, and sends many of them on to coveted colleges like MIT. Michael was also chosen as a Presidential Scholar while at Stuyvesant and later took some courses at Columbia University at the same time he was establishing himself as one of the top SAB students.

Few can live up to such a demanding and consuming schedule, though, or face the huge competitive pressures on all sides. Many dancers are noticeably uninterested in getting good high-school grades or in thinking about college. They want to dance, and when they are not dancing, they want to see dance, or take class, or do other dance-related things. That is their commitment; there is no room for anything else. Says Sean Lavery, "If you're going to do this ballet thing, you have to do it one hundred percent. Sometimes people ask me what I plan to do when I retire. It's impossible for me to think about what to do when performing is over; all I can think about is doing what I do. It's hard enough to get out there and make magic." He pauses, then laughs. "If I'd only had a better education, I could become a brain surgeon."

Some dancers don't bother going to a special school like PCS. They have tutors or finish high school by correspondence; some others take equivalency exams, and still others just abandon school altogether. Charlie Anderson dropped out of high school with the full blessing of his parents and his stepfather—all of whom were dancers. They understood that academics had no meaning for their son and that school interfered with what did mean something to him: dancing. They insisted that he read a list of books they'd put together for him, though. It included poetry and classics, and he loved all of it. Now Charlie dances with the New York City Ballet; high school never could have helped him get there.

That spring at Power, academic school was okay for Max; but PCS was the pits for Josh. What really mattered to them both was SAB, though, and that was getting better and better for Josh and worse and worse for Max, even though

Max had done a good job in *Nuts*. Back in December, his future had looked bright. He hadn't exactly stolen the show from Peter Martins, as he had planned to do, but he had performed with poise and had done the steps correctly. Max's mother thought that things were looking quite rosy for him and for her. Says Sean Lavery, looking back at the pint-size Candy-Cane, "He was terrific. He really could do anything."

By spring that was no longer true. His hip. What on earth was wrong with his hip? Why did it hurt so damn much, so damn much of the time? Why couldn't he do what he was used to doing? He went to doctors, therapists. No one seemed to know what was wrong. No two opinions were the same: growing pains, tendinitis, cysts, bone deterioration; on and on the diagnoses varied. So did the suggested remedies. Some just said rest. Max's father had a vitamin and nutritional solution. Surgery was mentioned, as was putting an end to dancing. Max was fifteen years old. He had just found the friends he wanted at SAB and had just become an official member of the select group that included Andrew and Eric, the truly cool older guys. They were not the most successful dancers at SAB, but they were certainly the Big Men on Campus, the girls' favorites, the party boys, the hell-raisers. These were the friends Max wanted; these were the people he wanted to be popular with. Now he was. And now he might have to give up dance, give up SAB, give up everything. His hip could make him lose it all.

When City Ballet principal Jock Soto was eleven years old, he had to leave SAB because of severe growing pains. He truly thought his life was over, that there was no hope for his future. At eleven. Five years later, he was a pro in the company. Max wasn't interested in anyone else, though. He didn't want to hear stories of others' successes or failures. He was obsessed by himself and by his hip. All he wanted was for the pain to stop, for the joint to get better, for things to get back to normal. He hurt, he didn't know why, and he was mad. Just as things were going his way in some areas, his body had to screw him up.

VI.

Girls

Max had always been on the withholding side. He didn't put himself out unless he wanted to. Ballet had come easily to him, and as for so many of the boys, so had ballet's treats: attention, acclaim, scholarships. Max didn't have to work too hard, and he gave no more than was required. If his attitude had needed a bit of work before, the pain only made it worse. As the aches and his dismay intensified, his effort in the studio diminished and his behavior worsened.

SAB teachers have great sympathy for injuries. They don't push students who are hurt, and they readily excuse them from taking class. It is a school rule, however, that students who don't dance in class stay and watch. For some that's a big help; they are still involved, and they can work things out in their minds if not their bodies; they can pretty well keep up with the group, at least mentally. For others, watching is torture. Max is from the latter school of thought. On the days when his hip hurt too much to take class, or enabled him only to take a portion of a class, he would try to watch, but usually he would end up leaving; he couldn't stand just sitting there.

Though SAB teachers do have great tolerance for injuries, they have no patience at all with goofing off and even less with breaking rules. Especially Richard Rapp. A hangnail gets his sympathy, but lack of interest, lack of effort, and rebellion all leave him totally cold. He feels that as a teacher, he must have control; he must have his students' full attention and energy; that that is the only way they will learn. He knows what his male students don't fully understand yet, that choosing to dance is choosing a hard life, that sacrifices only begin in class, that ballet will voraciously eat up all the time, energy, and devotion that the boys will be able to muster— forever. But he also knows that it is a privilege to be a practitioner of the oldest lively art, that the Poets of Gesture raise themselves to a very high level of humanity when they work hard at classical dance. He knows that dancing elevates one in more ways than just tours en l'air. Max hadn't a clue about any of this. He was miserable that his life was being so divided, that dancing, which used to be so much fun, was so difficult now, just at the time he was beginning to feel a part of the SAB scene, just as he felt he belonged there. He even had a girlfriend, his first.

Romy. She was the most beautiful girl Max had ever seen, and he had certainly been around his share of knock-outs. The classrooms and hallways of SAB brim over with young, delicate pulchritude. All the girls are pretty; some are ravishing. A few look more beautiful onstage than off, but there is not a single weed in the garden. It comes with the territory. Ballerinas are pretty. They dress in white or black leotards and often wear soft little chiffon skirts over them. Their long legs are swathed in pale tights and their toes covered with satin slippers. Topknots crown their shiny heads; earrings decorate their lobes, and eye makeup is part of the school uniform. These girls have been concentrating on looking beautiful, dancing beautifully, embodying beauty since they were about six years old. By fourteen, they have had considerable practice, and most do it very well. They move with speed and grace; their bodies are as slim and strong as young fillies', and their faces are animated.

Max had admired many lovelies in his dancing career, but Romy topped them all. And she liked him too. They went to parties together, and they sometimes danced together in partnering class. It was a very innocent romance, though, filled with yearning and soulful looks over cups of coffee in the cafeteria. But no sex. Max and Romy held hands and dreamed. Max wasn't at all ready for sex, not in any of its active guises, no matter how he pretended otherwise to his chums. He and Romy were like the idealized lovers in a ballet; it was very romantic, and she made his knees absolutely weak. It was pristine, virginal. It was wonderful.

Every week SAB boys get two chances to dance with the girls: in adagio, or partnering, class; and in social dancing, which fills one of the adagio time slots every other week. Peter Martins was a champion ballroom dancer as a child, even before he joined the School of the Royal Danish Ballet. When he took over as SAB faculty chief, the first thing he did was add social dancing classes to the curriculum for boys and girls over the age of fourteen. "Waltzing properly was a big help in my career," he says, "and I want these kids to have that advantage."

Social dancing at SAB bears no resemblance to what other American teens are learning at Miss So and So's School or in their high school gym. Those kids are learning how to touch-dance, are adding a waltz and a fox-trot to their list of social skills. At their lessons reluctant suited-up suitors and coy debs-to-be listen to advice about leading and following, about starting and stopping; then they take to the floor themselves: one-two-three; one-two-three; one-two-three. There are always knots of awkward boys slouching about the sidelines, making fun of the girls and never daring to take one in their arms and attempt to move their feet at the same time. Unbid-for girls cluster embarrassedly together at the dance floor's edge until a ladies' choice is called for; then they uninhibitedly race to the partner of their choice and grab themselves a chance to float and dream.

The dancing that SAB kids learn does not prepare them for cotillions or proms or country club *thé dansants*. They learn how to ballroom dance onstage, in front of an audience. They learn how to waltz and tango and two-step like professionals, and they learn from professionals. City Ballet dancer Diana White regularly glides divinely in Balanchine's *Vienna Waltzes*. Laughing, she recalls the Christmas dance when she and her boyfriend were asked to start off the proceedings with a waltz. "We just tripped all over each other," she says. "How you waltz onstage is *soooo* different from how you do it on a dance floor."

For social dancing classes girls wear shoes with heels and wrap diaphanous skirts around their workaday leotards. They dab on a little extra makeup and add long, sparkling earrings to their costumes, some with stars dangling at the bottom. Occasionally they even wear lace-patterned tights for additional glamour. The boys don their basic non-ballet-class uniforms: usually jeans, shirts, sweaters, sneakers. Only one boy keeps his slippers and tights on, adding just a sweat-shirt—Nilas Martins, newly arrived from Denmark and the son of the Boss. There are many more girls than boys. Some of the boys, like Ben from Belgium, have three partners at one time; while he dances with one, the other two do their parts alongside, arms resting gently on imaginary princes' shoulders and palms. Max and his chum Brandon, who call the class "social disease," clown around with their partners and with each other, bumping accidentally on purpose and fairly dusting the floor with mock-Astaire dips.

The class is taught by Pierre Dulaine and Yvonne Marceau. They demonstrate, dancing as one, smooth and soft as a cat's belly, with crisp turns and never a trodden toe. They make it look very easy, which it decidedly is not. The students try to imitate the steps. "Ouch," goes the cry, and Pierre feigns a fit. Clapping his hands to stop the pianist and then raising them in shocked disbelief, he cries, "No, no, no, no, no. You never start forward on your right foot. Never. It is always your left." During some fancy Latin moves he rhythmically reminds the girls to "follow your toes with your nose. Remember, your nose follows your toes." One boy bends over in pain; his knees ache agonizingly from these movements, which are so different from ballet. Two girls dance together, alternating turns at being Ginger Rogers.

The very first of these classes was taught by Martins himself, with Suzanne Farrell as his partner, and Pierre and Yvonne as spectators. Every eligible student showed up to take the class, and many others were strewn about the room to watch. The studio was crammed to overflowing, and Suzanne was late. By the time she arrived, Peter had begun the class and had lines of couples waltzing toward him on a diagonal. Suzanne arrived and disappeared into the crowd at the back of the room, soon to come waltzing by on the arm of one of the boys. Martins pretended not to notice her, so she went back to the group and tried it again with another of the boys. By this time the whole room was atwitter with giggles and

Peter Martins, teaching the first-ever social dancing class at SAB.

nervous expectation. Finally Martins mimed an exaggerated shock and surprise at seeing his former partner, then gave her a true cavalier's welcome, bowing from the waist and offering his huge hand in a gesture that was absolute poetry. As she accepted with her special grace and gracefulness, chills ran up and down the students' spines, and they issued a collective sigh.

Things quickly settled down to business, with all the young dancers extra-inspired to work even harder at trying to look like the god and goddess in the room with them, the two who are human enough to let the acolytes call them by their first names. Suzanne and Peter first danced together, demonstrating, then they each danced with some of the students, which added a special excitement and tension to the proceedings. Finally Peter started to show the boys how to hold the girls by assuming the girl's part himself and having some of the boys hold him and lead him. Barely stifled gasps and snickers filled the room. One of the boys said afterward of cavorting with his hero, "Wow. That was awful. I was terrified."

In adagio class the boys and girls dance ballet together. They practice the age-old steps they will one day do onstage; they become the partner and the partnered. Girls learn to trust that their partners will be there when they need them, and boys learn to live up to that trust. They learn how to support an arabesque, how to lift and catch a girl, how to stop a pirouetting princess so that she faces the audience, and how to present her to their public as though she is the most important jewel in his collection. Adagio class is where the boys get experience in handling girls, and where girls get used to being handled. Before class begins, the hornier boys hang out in the hall, comparing notes on dancing with the curvier girls. During class the studio comes alive with sexuality, as do the dancers. There is extreme, if public, intimacy in adagio class. All in the line of work, bodies collide and girls drape themselves over the boys. The partners hold on closely and gaze deep into each other's eyes. Girls are grasped by their upper thighs, or lifted just under their arms, where male fingers can hardly avoid quick feels. Imaginations run wild, and romances get kindled in adagio class.

Animosity can rear its rather homely head here too. These young girls and boys become working couples in this class; it is a difficult relationship at best. Understanding and cooperation are supposed to be the key words, but everyone here wants to be the Star, and egos can rage as loudly as hormones. Sometimes couples compete with each other as much as with the rest of the twosomes swirling around. Girls can get testy, can snap at their young princes for small imperfections; sometimes they even blame the boys for mistakes they have made themselves. Princes can have their revenge, though, can seize the upper hand, can occasionally even upstage their precious princesses. When Peter Martins teaches adagio, he encourages the boys to "show her who's the boss." When Richard Rapp teaches, he pretends the same oblivion to both wooing and warfare between the sexes.

The confidence about their bodies and about touching and being touched that adagio classes instill in young ballet dancers makes them seem older than their "civilian" compatriots; so do their intense motivation and discipline. But if dancers develop these adult traits early, they are also kept children in many ways. Many aspects of "real life" don't touch them, so they also somehow seem a great deal younger than their counterparts. Max seemed suave and sophisticated as he held Romy in a fish dive or sat her high up on his shoulder. He seemed very at ease with physicality and sexuality, but that ease ended at the door of SAB.

Like so many American males, Max had his first tentative sexual experience not with his girlfriend, Romy, but with someone else. Edward Villella ran a two-week dance camp on Cape Cod that summer. Max was given a scholarship and went in spite of his nagging hip. "It was the best time I ever had in my life," he now says wistfully. He wasn't there a full week before his hip gave in totally and he was unable to dance. Maybe that was part of the reason he had such a good time. He stayed down on the Cape until the camp ended, so he had many hours to spend at the beach getting to know all the beauties who were there. And to try out his burgeoning manhood. She wasn't Romy, but that's what he had in mind.

All they did was neck, but it was a new, delightful, and somewhat embarrassing experience for Max. That's why he wanted it to be someone other than Romy; he couldn't, wouldn't, be foolish with her. He practiced a variety of different ways to kiss until he found a style he thought particularly suited him; then he decided his future was looking brighter, after all, and he couldn't wait to get home to his real girl.

Suddenly Max's summer was over prematurely. It was decided that the only solution for his hip—the diagnosis at this point was a cyst—was surgery to remove the offending mass and to get the boy back to the barre. He came back to New York and entered Columbia Presbyterian Hospital, his terror mixed with fascination for the quiet, high-tech feel of the place, for the buttons to be pushed and the bed that could be adjusted so many ways, and for all the attention he was getting. The nurses doted on him, flirted with him, and were clearly impressed that he was a ballet dancer. His mother fussed over him and brought him flowers. Romy came to visit, too, held his hand and looked sweetly and caringly into his eyes. All he had to do was lie there. His hip didn't even hurt when he lay down, and now he didn't have to try, try to get that joint to do what he asked of it in spite of the pain. That night, after everyone had gone home, he felt like a little kid again. Then the first thing he knew, it was five in the morning and they were getting him ready for the operation. "Wait a minute," he wanted to say. "Just slow down. Remember, I'm only fifteen years old. I have a long and bright future ahead of me, don't I?" Then a needle jabbed his arm, and his cares started to melt away. By the time he was rolling down the hall on the gurney, he was also floating away on a tranquilized cloud.

Pain is the companion of all dancers. Jacques d'Amboise danced for years on webbed feet. Decades of abuse had so crippled his toes with arthritis that finally the "knuckles" had to be removed and the digits sewn together for balance. Sean Lavery and Mikhail Baryshnikov have both had their knees operated on, and Rudolf Nureyev's feet are grotesquely gnarled and misshapen. Fifteen is very young for surgery, though. All dancers pay a bodily toll for constantly doing what doesn't come naturally, but usually the problems of teenagers have more to do with growth or pulled muscles or shin splints. Every time a sixteen-year-old boy shoots up another inch, his new height gobbles up all his weight and strength, and he has to grow into his body once again. NYCB member Brian Reeder recalls when he was at SAB, eighteen years old, 6'1½", and still growing. "My main problem was gaining strength. Every time I thought I was getting there with a certain muscle, I grew, and the muscle stretched."

Minor injuries abound at SAB, and aches and pains proliferate. Because of the competition, though, many youngsters make the mistake of not listening to their bodies, not tending to injuries while they are still minor. Refusing to miss a class, or even to admit to injury is a kind of dancers' machismo that, like almost any other kind of machismo, usually leads to trouble. SAB students eventually find a favorite chiropractor, physical therapist, or sports medicine expert, and there is a sign-up sheet on the school bulletin board for appointments with the company doctor. Students are not supposed to visit the NYCB's physical therapist, but many sneak over to her, anyhow, and she is generous about dealing with them. She understands the risks they take, and so do SAB staffers.

Comments Lincoln Kirstein, "Dancers are always in

hazard, but they get to know their bodies through injury. Maybe the only way to really understand their bodies is by hurt. It's hard, but they have to go through it, and they come out stronger at the other end . . . if they come out." He continues, "Dancers are always in doubt. They need moral strength to bear it. Our students know a lot more about life than most kids. We teach what the high schools and colleges don't teach. They learn about success, failure, suffering, injury. Surgery is not an injury, though. It's a tragedy."

VII.

Frustration

Publicly Max made light of his operation. It wasn't so tough, he claimed, and he was. Privately he wasn't so sure. During August's sultry, heavy-aired, fry-an-egg-on-the-sidewalk New York City days, he hobbled about on crutches. It was tough. It was hot. It was miserable, and it hurt. Then September rolled around, and it was back-to-school time. Max became a boy without a country, with no place to go. He had not healed well enough to take dance class for a few more weeks, and the school he had come to enjoy, Power Memorial, was closed up tight, never to reopen, a victim of its financial times and hungry real-estate developers. His brother had moved to Albuquerque and would be going to school there; his sister went to the all-girls Sacred Heart across town. Even if he'd been able to convince his mother to let him go to PCS, there was no money for tuition, and she didn't trust any of the public schools. So he went on correspondence.

A few other SAB students were taking the Wisconsin University correspondence courses. For the highly motivated it's a real answer to the academic dilemma. Not having to attend classes or conform to a traditional school setting gives the dancing high-schoolers the time and freedom to pursue their careers and to do their academic studies when they can fit them in. For the unmotivated, correspondence school can be a trap. Each student is supposed to have an adult who supervises him or her, who sees that the work is done on some sort of schedule, in the correct order, and that it is mailed off in time to get graded and be granted the proper credit. There was no such person in Max's life. Sometimes his mother would decide to seize control. She would close him in his room for study time; she would carry on about how hard he must work, but then she would get distracted. Consistency had never been her longest suit. She didn't even want it to be; it wasn't exciting enough, and it reeked of cooperation, collaboration, acceptance of traditional values. She would have none of that.

So Max did his homework only occasionally and never got around to sending any of it in. He tried to sit through the dance classes he could not yet take, but that was impossible. When he stayed, he ended up clowning around, making faces at the other dancers, and finally leaving just before the teacher asked him to depart.

Max had grown some over the summer; he was 5'4" now, short, but more of an appropriate height for his age. His growth had all been from the waist up, though. His legs seemed to be getting shorter and shorter. What is wanted, of course, is for a dancer's legs to stretch out long and graceful, to strongly support the upper body and elegantly move him about. This wasn't happening for Max. He couldn't really believe what was happening to him—and not happening for him. It was just a few months ago that he thought he really had a grip on things. Then he lost that grasp; his world was starting to spin out of control.

At first Max's teachers were very sympathetic toward him. Krammie would laugh with him, imitate him, hobble around a little in empathy, and pat him supportively on the shoulder, hoping to give the youngster courage and encouragement. Mr. Rapp was gentle; he tried to help the maimed boy ease his way back, tried to show him how to build up his strength again without risking further injury. And Max tried to listen, tried to cooperate, but he couldn't stand it. He had lost so much ground. What used to be tricky was now hard; what used to be barely doable was now impossible. He heard the same corrections day after day after day, and he still couldn't incorporate them into his work. Depressed, he lounged around SAB's halls all day, supposedly doing his correspondence homework but actually just hanging out, and he felt less and less cool all the time . . . and angrier and angrier.

All of Max's older brothers and sisters were now in Albuquerque. The oldest, Lana, had married and moved there, and the others followed one at a time. That left Max and Brenda at home with their mother, which meant that her full attention was directed at them all the time. Brenda Fuqua is reminiscent of Amanda, the mother in Tennessee Williams's *The Glass Menagerie*. Attractive if a little too round— "After fourteen years I've still got baby fat from giving birth to Brenda," she will explain—she must have been a lovely-looking young woman. When she reminisces and talks about her childhood, she remembers how her mother would brush the daughter's hair for long, happy hours and what a considerate woman she was, how she always remembered the thoughtful gesture, gift, or note. Says the daughter without regret, "I'm the opposite." Brenda talks of tiptoeing around her Louisiana home in the afternoons when her father was napping, of being looked after by black family retainers who were once convicts, of an arranged marriage she had to accept although she was really in love with another boy.

You can almost see her taking out a ball gown, holding it up to her body, and waltzing around the living room, as Amanda would do, talking about the "gentleman callers" she had had as a girl.

Like Amanda, Brenda is obsessed, and also like Amanda, her children are the objects of her obsession. Still, she is scattershot, quixotic; her obsessions can be easily spent. She describes herself as a Christian, qualifying, "Not the kind that can't drink wine or do anything else. I believe that Christianity frees you to do what you want." Like Amanda also, Brenda struggles to keep her family solvent; financially they swing from flush to broke regularly, as commissions come in and get used up, and as Max's father sends or does not send checks. Amanda called all the ladies in town to try to sell them magazine subscriptions; Brenda Fuqua mowed her neighbors' lawns for money in Dallas and is now slugging it out in the world of Manhattan real estate, a tough, grabby, shadowy community where nothing is certain and everything is subject to negotiation, rule bending, and deal making.

Her rules for her children are many; hours are rigid and freedoms hard to come by. Her paranoia about giving them more rope is noted by all who know them. Basic living, though, meals and laundry and homework, are pretty much laissez-faire; everyone fends for himself. Max fixes his own breakfast and lunch, and he has brought his dirty laundry to SAB more than once because he didn't get it done during the hours his building's laundry room is open.

Brenda is a dreamer. Her apartment is in chaos,

Brenda Fuqua, watching her son take class.

clothes and papers and things everywhere, everything un-
dusted, a litter box for the two cats unchanged in weeks, a
sink piled high with dirty dishes. She barely notices. She has
no room of her own; her things are scattered, and at night she
unfolds a futon and sleeps on the dining room floor. Her

daughter has a tiny, curtained-off space that was once a pantry or maid's room. Max has the one bedroom in the apartment; it's big and outfitted with furniture specially bought for him. Originally he had to share the space with Stephen; now he has it all to himself. His clothes cover the floor, paperbacks are strewn all over, and the bed has not been made up for as long as anyone can remember.

Brenda talks about classier times; her eyes, which are usually alert and steely, soften as she describes happiness, both past and future. Her personal plans include living in Europe and accumulating a variety of advanced college degrees. She is fueled with fantasy, but she is not a woman to be underestimated. She's made it to New York, hasn't she? She may make some of her other dreams come true as well.

The Thanksgiving after Max's operation, Brenda felt sick and tired of feeling sick and tired. She needed a treat; she needed to avoid the holiday, and Max needed a little uplifting too. Maybe if he saw some other ballet and took a class or two at some other school, he would feel better. She had never been out of the United States, and she had always pined to travel. It was time. With her handy-dandy American Express card she booked flights, packed up the kids, and off they went to London. Mother Brenda loved it. Daughter Brenda thought it was okay. Max was less enthusiastic. He would have liked to stay in New York. However, as luck would have it, seated next to him on the flight over was Alexander Goudonov, the Bolshoi defector who was dancing with ABT and who has since made a name for himself as a vibrant movie star. Though he couldn't exactly have been called effusive toward Max, they did chat a bit, and when the little Texan deplaned in England, he felt like all-American hot stuff. Once there, though, he wanted to forget about dance. He didn't see any other company, and he never took a class anywhere. He became a tourist. He went sightseeing and shopping, and he walked and walked and walked. Soon, very soon, the vacation ended, the family returned, and Max was back at SAB.

As the weeks wore on, he seemed to get more and more confused, more and more rebellious, less and less interested in what he was doing. His correspondence courses mostly went unlooked at; only occasionally did he do any of the lessons, and then only half- or even "quarter-heartedly." When he appeared in dance class, he was always clad in some violation of the dress code: Hard Rock Cafe T-shirt, sweats on over his tights, sweatshirt wrapped around his waist or shoulder, watch always on his wrist (no matter how many times he was told by Mr. Rapp that sporting a watch in ballet class was as inappropriate as "wearing your shoes in the shower"), and slippers that were usually falling apart. That was when he appeared; often he was a no-show. As long as it was anywhere near warm enough, he hung out in the park, drinking beer out of a brown bag, pretending that SAB didn't exist.

Says Max, "I know I didn't go all out. Partially it was my hip. They thought I was just being lazy and screwing around." Pause. "I guess half the time I was. I didn't like their being so big in my life and taking up all my time. I wanted more friends and more of a normal life. I wanted to feel like I didn't have to go to class and that it wasn't wrong to stay with my friends."

At home Max was sullen, silent, and gone as often as possible. The more his mother would nag, the more distant and disobeying—and rude—he would become. It wasn't like him. He had always been sweet-natured, except for that temper. Everywhere Max looked, it seemed to him that they were after him with rules and rules and rules, most of them stupid and just meant to remind him that he was nothing, that others had full control of his life and he had none. He was sick of it; he was furious, and there was no one he could talk to about it. With his friends he kept up a brave and sassy front, bragging about his lack of respect and refusal to comply with anyone's directions. He drank as much beer as he could, and he was as resistant to authority as he could possibly be.

One day in March, Max was sitting in front of the school, wondering what to do next, where to go, when along came the revered Andrew on his bicycle. Class was over; it was after seven o'clock in the evening, and Max was expected home. Instead he leapt onto the back of Drew's bike and off they rushed to the most cooperative deli, the one where underage teens could always buy some beer. They got a quart each and zoomed over to Central Park, where they drank and rode around until after eleven o'clock. To Max it felt great, as though he were living dangerously.

In fact he was, but nothing untoward happened, except that his mother was in a fit when he got home at almost midnight without ever having called. After that she did all she could to control her boy. She would stop in at school unexpectedly to see if he was there, and for a time she insisted upon picking him up after class and escorting him home every day. He was humiliated, but it didn't work. Not even the threat to send him back to Texas to live with his father really had any effect on Max. Publicly he was a little rebel, in total revolt. Privately he was a mess and getting worse.

A couple of weeks later, a spring day appeared with a promise in the air that was too much for Max. T. S. Eliot was wrong, March can also be a damned cruel month. All our losses and potential losses slap us in the face as the season of renewal tentatively begins. Max couldn't take his anymore, and he was not going to take Josh anymore, either. Josh was tall and getting taller; he was liked by all his teachers, and he got lots of positive attention. Max had had it. So, one day in class he sent forth the punch that rocked the halls, and then he went off to exile.

VIII.

Second Chance

During his two-week probation Max did nothing. He lay about his room. He read fantasy books by day and watched anything at all on television until late at night. He smoked countless cigarettes, hanging out the window of his bedroom so that his mother couldn't smell the smoke. He walked in the park some, but slowly, aimlessly. He sat on park benches. He moped. He thought and thought and came up with no answers. So he stopped thinking. He never took one class at any other ballet school. He didn't exercise; he didn't even stretch. He didn't do any of his correspondence school homework. He didn't clean his room, hang up his clothes, or do his laundry. It was his most complete immersion in passivity. It was as though he spent the fourteen days sleepwalking. Max didn't know where he was going or what he wanted. He was fifteen years old. He felt a thousand and he felt three. All he'd done his whole life, since he was seven years old, was dance. His dancing made his mother proud, and that made him feel happy, worthwhile, and safe. And in charge. After all, who had gotten them out of Highland Park? Who had brought them to New York? His mother's hopes were pinned on him. And now what?

Happier days
in Dallas.

Life was so hard now. The ballet that had been such a joy when he was very young was now the source of so much pain, physical and emotional. Max thought back to his days in Texas, when he was just a little kid performing with the Dallas Metropolitan Ballet and actually taking company class with all the adults. "They all thought I was so cute; I was like their little mascot. There was one woman, though, the most beautiful woman I have ever seen," he says with a sigh. "She used to sit me on her lap all the time and fuss over me. I was her pet. That was really great." After thinking for a minute he remembers dreamily, "There's a certain smell. I can't describe it, but it's the smell of the theater in Dallas where we danced. Whenever I smell that smell, I just want to be back in that theater."

What would be waiting for Max back at SAB? Had he spoiled his chances there forever? Would he ever get promoted to Advanced Men's? Would he ever be in Special, or would he be blackballed from progressing, no matter how hard he tried? Would he get a part in the all-important spring workshop performance, the rite of passage between school and the pros? Or would he be relegated permanently to the abandoned, the forgotten, the going-nowhere hangers-on? It was so unfair, he thought. He was a better dancer than many who had been promoted already, he thought.

When the day rolled around for Max to leave his limbo and rejoin the living, he was relieved and also apprehensive. Everyone in the school knew what had happened. It had escaped no one. Some of the other boys thought Max was terrific—a few had wanted to paste Josh one themselves. Others were as shocked as Mrs. Gleboff. Some of the girls were scandalized but intrigued. Most of the younger ones had crushes on Max already; to them his newfound reputation for violence only increased his mystery and appeal. Walking from the bus to school, Max worked on assuming his usual response to fear and the unknown. He tried to look slightly preoccupied, superior, cool, bored, even a little macho. It was easy; he'd had lots of practice. He strolled, seemingly nonchalant, through the door and down the hall, hoping no one could hear the pounding of his heart, working hard to control the quaking that was beginning in his knees and spreading throughout his entire body.

It couldn't be! The first person he saw! She was coming right toward him. Help! There was no way to avoid her. Oh, God! It was Madame Danilova, the legendary ballerina, now an octogenarian and an important part of the very soul of SAB. Always referred to by just her last name, Alexandra Danilova is a bit of living ballet history. She grew up in Imperial Russia with Georgi Balanchivadze; she left her motherland with him in 1925, lived with him in Europe, and worked with him there and here. For more than two decades she toured America coast to coast as the prima ballerina of the Ballet Russe de Monte Carlo, making her farewell appearance in New York in 1957, and she has been teaching at SAB since 1964. Danilova is a walking encyclopedia of ballets by the great Franco-Russian choreographer Petipa (*Swan Lake, Sleeping Beauty,* etc.) and has often been called upon to help stage works from her memory. Ballet is learned in the body, with the mind's help and the memory's collusion. Recording ballets, whether by notation or videotape, is an inexact science. Danilova is a better repository; her mind is filled with steps; her body remembers them too. When she teaches class, as she still does every day, several times a day, she still demonstrates, bending, reaching and turning with a hint, like the pentimento of a painting, of the glories of her younger days.

In the halls and studios of SAB, Danilova is an elegant and charming symbol of all that is good about ballet. Graceful and slim, with still beautiful legs, glamorous in her mascara, blue eye shadow, and professionally coiffed golden hair, she was swathed, on Max's fateful day, in spangled apricot chiffon over her apricot leotard. The color was perfect; she looked as

Madame
Alexandra
Danilova.

though a peachy sunrise had just washed over her. The embodiment of the steel fist in the chamois glove, Danilova is not just peaches and cream, however. She is a tough teacher who does not easily suffer lack of attention or unwillingness to work. Preparing students for a workshop performance, she can be heard scolding a young ballerina emphatically, "You must do work on your own. You cannot simply go from rehearsal to rehearsal!" Then she will impatiently query a group, "How many times do I have to tell you? The arabesque should be to the corner! The Italian way is straight, the French diagonal. Monsieur Petipa was a Frenchman, so it is to the corner! Now, again . . ." Her curtness sends shivers down the spines of many an SAB student.

And here she was. Would Max's bad luck never end? Oh, well, might as well face it. He walked toward her, trying to look confident, smiling just a little. She approached him, stopped, looked him square in the eye, and said, "*Weelll, eet's the leetle foojeeteef*," with a conspiratorial twinkle and a pat on the arm. A last-second reprieve from the governor could not have meant more to a prisoner heading for the gallows than that understanding, lighthearted welcome from Madame meant to Max.

During her years of performing throughout the United States, more than one generation of Americans got to witness Alexandra Danilova's special insouciance. She has legions of lifelong fans. That April day she added a new devotee to her long list, and she did so without moving so much as a toe.

Mr. Rapp wasn't nearly as welcoming, and even Krammie was distant; both felt Max had to prove himself all over again. Their disapproval of, and distaste for, his violent display were very apparent. Max was going to have to make good with these two, and to do so he was going to have to work very hard. That's what they thought. He wasn't about to. He was tired of their disapproval; he was tired of always having to prove himself. He was tired of looking in the mirror all the time, of constantly staring at himself, seeing what he could and could not do, tired of watching himself do it incorrectly or semi-correctly or sometimes very well, but not often enough.

Max was unnerved by having everyone know everything about him, tired of having everything show so damn much. There was no privacy at SAB, none at all. In class there was no way to hide. Height, weight, ability, inability, anger, and confusion were all evident to everyone and all staring back from that omnipresent mirror. Max did his best to appear at ease, but he wasn't. He was very unhappy. He didn't even bother trying to see Romy anymore. What was the point? His closest friend at the moment, the only person who understood, was Ann. She was going through her own horrible time, and the two commiserated. Max was not growing tall enough, and Ann had grown too tall. She had lost all her strength, and she was almost too tall even to be a ballet dancer. Her dancing was rapidly falling apart, and she was not so keen on academic school, either. Ann was sharing an apartment in the city with Peter, a close friend of Max's, in a platonic relationship. She was older than Max but too young and not together enough to be living away from home. Peter worried about her constantly. That annoyed her. Ann didn't want all the responsibility she had for herself, and she didn't want him to mother her. She wanted to go home and be a part of her family again, but she was afraid to admit it. It sounded like defeat. She was as confused as Max, and the two offered as much comfort to each other as possible, while their lives swirled about them.

One day Ann's parents came into the city from their suburban home and stopped by PCS to see how their daughter was doing. They had been concerned; she seemed troubled. Their fears were confirmed when they discovered that Ann was not at school. She was often not at school, they were told. Whatever it was she was doing and how she was doing, she was doing it somewhere else. Next her parents called SAB. No Ann. They were getting very nervous. They rang her apartment, and there she was, in the middle of the day. They went right over, had a talk with her, and took her home. She was very relieved. Ann looked mature, and she felt she at least had to seem grown-up. Inside, though, she was a scared kid who needed her parents. They told her she could quit ballet anytime she wanted, and they got her to see a therapist. She's much happier now. She stayed with the doctor and she stayed with dance. She also continued to stay at home.

Max didn't have the same options as Ann. There was no one to scoop him up and make him safe. He wanted to quit dancing; he could have used a therapist. Instead he talked to his mother, which he felt was as helpful. "She should be your best friend," he says. Brenda convinced her son not to leave SAB, not to let them force him to quit, to tough it out and not give in to what they both believed was harassment.

There was no out for Max. He was trapped. Once again, though, being a male worked in his favor. Male dancers are still rare enough that they get preferential treatment rarely offered to girls. Just weeks after he "lost it" and resorted to violence to express himself, Max learned that he had been granted a full scholarship for the summer session at the San Francisco Ballet School. And what's more, his father agreed to pay for his airfare. Even Max could hardly believe his good fortune; it was almost too good to be true. This was salvation; this was freedom. This was going to save his neck and maybe even his career. He would be getting out of town, three thousand miles out. And six other boys from SAB were also going. Andrew would be there, and Rob too. Yes, and even Josh. Mark had left SAB, had decided to study elsewhere; he was the only one of Max's friends who wasn't going west. San Francisco was the place to be this summer. Once again Max would be with the right group. He'd be away from his mother and her controls and rules and threats. He'd be away from SAB and its insistence on no leg warmers and no writing on your T-shirt and no watches and no ankle showing and no this and no that and Mr. Rapp's disapproving glances and Krammie's shaking head. And he'd be away from being on time and being there day after day and tendu and plié and plié and tendu and getting nowhere and nowhere and nowhere. Max was getting another chance.

Every summer aspiring dancers travel from their "home" schools to study with other teachers, to be seen by different choreographers and company heads, to increase their skills and their options. The schools get a look at large numbers of new dancers for a period of several weeks. SAB brings two hundred and fifty different students in just for the summer; a few are invited to stay. The cross-pollination that used to be limited to Europe, Denmark, and Russia now reaches around the world, and its hub is here in America, where students rush each summer north and south, east and west, sometimes to more than one locale. Though there is no cultural exchange of dance students between the U.S. and the U.S.S.R. as yet, Europeans come here regularly. European companies have also offered performing homes to scores of American dancers—so many, in fact, that the balance of trade in dancers has shifted dramatically. America now exports more ballet dancers than she imports, and schools here welcome students from as near as Canada and as far away as South America, Japan, China, and India. The Royal Danish Ballet School used to be shut tight to outsiders, no matter how gifted, but now that alumnus Peter Martins is the head of SAB, balletic detente between America and Denmark has become established. Handpicked American students now spend summers practicing Bournonville technique in Copenhagen, and several tall, blond Scandinavians can be spotted in classes at SAB and onstage with the NYCB—including one Nilas Martins, Peter's talented son, who is somewhat reluctantly following in his father's slippers.

It was Ford Foundation money, largely administered

by SAB, that was responsible for spreading quality ballet teaching in the United States. In fact, it was Ford's monetary commitment in the sixties that paved the way for the ballet boom of the seventies. Ford scholars were found, fostered, and funded all over the country, either to stay in their own communities and study there, under the guidance of SAB personnel, or to come to New York on scholarship. One of the very first Ford students was a girl from Cincinnati named Roberta Sue Ficker. She soon hypnotized Balanchine and the rest of the world as Suzanne Farrell, merely the finest ballerina of her time, and a continuing inspiration to countless younger dancers, both male and female.

On the West Coast the San Francisco Ballet School received Ford scholars as well, and the two academies were given real national status with direct Ford grants in 1963. Each received enough money to concentrate on giving the most talented students in the country the most complete classical ballet training. Earlier it regularly became a difficult decision whether to turn away some klunk who could come up with the full price of lessons. Now all energies could be devoted to preparing professional dancers, to creating an ever deeper reservoir of fully able performers to nourish the New York City Ballet and the San Francisco company as well—and, as it turns out, many other companies here and abroad. Funds were promised for a full decade, just about the exact amount of time it takes to prepare a professional ballet dancer.

For ten years the two academies flourished, expanded, increased their teaching staffs, and lengthened their lists of distinguished alumni. Then—suddenly, it seemed—the time was up and the money stopped. The ending of Ford's financial aid precipitated a huge monetary crisis for the West Cost school and company; the problem was deepened and intensified by some serious mismanagement. By the fall of 1974, bankruptcy loomed large for both the San Francisco Ballet and the School. The day was saved only by an extensive campaign to raise money that was begun by the dancers.

Five hundred thousand dollars had to be raised in eleven days, or the doors would be closed. Out went the rallying cry—S.O.B., Save Our Ballet. Dancers took to the streets, performed in shop windows, at a football game half-time, and even at Marine World. They took to the telephones, too, hunting down prospective angels and earning many donations and much nationwide press attention. Future company director Michael Smuin, who had just come back from ABT in 1973, did his share of PR work as well, even entering a local tricycle race and winning by beating a chimpanzee. More important, though, he took their case to state and federal officials. Between money gathered five dollars at a time and a National Endowment of the Arts grant of $40,000, the public's consciousness was raised, and membership in the San Francisco Ballet Association quickly soared to two thousand from a mere three hundred. By the middle of October the necessary funds had been obtained, and the company and school were saved—by a nose. *Dancemagazine* said at the time, "San Francisco Ballet has come closer to dissolution than any surviving American dance company. Its saga should be written as 'The Company That Wouldn't Die.' "

When Ford withdrew its funding from SAB, everyone thought, "It's over; the school's finished," according to former director of special events Mary Porter. "No one at the school knew how to raise money," she says. "We'd never raised a single dollar before." Panicked SAB officials convinced Ford to give them a withdrawal grant; the weaning would include lessons in fiscal responsibility. Funds would come in descending amounts, and the school would have to make up the difference between the Ford money and their budget requirements. The first year the school was responsible for raising $100,000. They called upon reliable and moneyed friends and managed to gather $60,000, but they didn't know what to do about the rest. They had an ace in the hole that their western counterparts sadly lacked, however, in the name of George Balanchine. For years Rudolf Nureyev had been asking Mr. Balanchine if he could dance the master's *Apollo*, a danseur's star vehicle to music by Stravinsky. Always the answer was no. The year the school needed $40,000, Nureyev was to appear with a little company he had put together called Nureyev and Friends. Once again he asked Mr. Balanchine if he could dance *Apollo*. This time the answer was, "Yes—for a fee of $40,000." Nureyev grabbed at the chance, anted up the money, and Balanchine turned it right over to the school. The $100,000 was raised.

Needless to say, SAB could not continue to count on such luck, so they learned their fund-raising lessons very well indeed. The SAB development staff now gathers huge amounts of dollars yearly. Says Porter, "It took us three years back then in the seventies—and we didn't meet the Ford goals all the time—but we learned." In 1978, the real turning point was reached, and the event took place that made SAB number one, the official American academy of ballet. The National Endowment gave them a special matching grant, the first to be given to any school of any kind of dance. "They turned us around from the nervous stage," says Porter.

SAB and SFBS have always been sister schools, and just as sisters compete for friends and beaux, the East and West Coast ballet establishments often vie for top young dancers. If it's not quite the Ivy League, and if the wooing is not quite as intense as the pursuit of the hottest high-school hoopster—with offers of money, cars, clothes, girls, and anything else the giant wants if he will just come and sink buckets for Ole Blue or Ole Whatever—still the competition can heat up. Especially for boys.

Full scholarships are commonplace for the lads; a living allowance is often added, and sometimes academic school tuition is thrown in for good measure. Boys with real potential get offers that would bring tears to the large eyes of most struggling baby ballerinas. Over the last decade and a half or so, there has been a very large increase in the number of American boys studying dance, but there still is, and probably always will be, a shortage of the really gifted, and those special few are pursued with real vigor. SAB is the strongest magnet; it pulls in the greatest number of talented boys because it offers stronger male teaching and has the funds to supply what the boys need. SAB can now afford to turn down or release males with little promise or lack of interest, and lure and keep those with the greatest ability and future. Says former SFBS Director Richard Cammack (whose own stepson is SAB graduate Charlie Anderson), "We just can't compete with SAB for boys. We can offer them scholarships and stipends, but they can top that with airfare to and from. And remember, we're dealing with the male ego here."

The San Francisco Ballet and School have a whole snazzy new building of their own. They moved in in 1983; it's an impressive facility. There are three floors of studios; there is a dancers' lounge and other comforts not of home. SAB has a part of a floor of the Juilliard Building. SAB boys are always impressed with San Francisco's "plant," but usually a little less so after they have taken a few classes in SFBS's smaller studios, where they don't have the same floor space to cover.

San Francisco summer students are housed in USF dormitories, where they have the same kind of fun kids at camp enjoy. They short-sheet each other's beds; they make a pile of all the furniture in someone's room; they stay up all night long and make noise in spite of the many warnings from the adults in charge; and they have weekly beach parties with the girls who have come west from schools around the country. They also get lessons in character dancing and take some modern and jazz classes—all of which are off-limits back home in New York. It's a real holiday for the Easterners, even though they work hard at their dance lessons, and it's all paid for by someone else.

Lots of boys from SAB head west every summer, as Max was getting ready to do, and sample the delights of San Francisco's ballet world. They always have a great time. Max intended to have the best summer any of them had ever had at any time over the years of the exchange. This trip was the most important journey of his life to date, he thought, and he planned to make the most of it—whatever that meant.

IX.

Roots

The close balletic ties between SAB and San Francisco will probably tighten even further in the years to come, now that former NYCB star Helgi Tomasson is director of the San Francisco company, but he is just the latest link between the two. The history of the relationship is a long one and an integral part of the development of ballet in America, particularly ballet for men.

It is not accidental that male dancing has now come of age in the United States. Neoclassicism and the American male were meant for each other. Says former City Ballet dancer Edward Villella, "It used to be that ballet was based on nineteenth-century romanticism, which was foreign to Americans. But now we have neoclassicism, thanks to Balanchine and other American geniuses like Robbins, Graham, and Paul Taylor. Neoclassicism is filled with American dignity, elegance, nobility. It has sharp, clear, quick lines. You should watch a Russian try to dance *Agon*!"

Neoclassicism didn't just spring up, however; it evolved out of all that had come before it. Long before neoclassicism, long before nineteenth-century romanticism, and even long before America, there was classical dance, and the male dancer always had a vital role to play in its growth and development.

Before people sang, they danced. They danced for religious reasons; they danced in joy and in sorrow, to ask for peace and to prepare for war. Dance has always been an integral part of humanity and as vital to our survival as air, or sunlight, or food and water. The roots of classical dance go way back, too, not to the earliest times, but as far back as the choruses of the ancient Greek tragedies. Dance was a key method of communication in the plays, one clearer and less ambiguous than words. In Roman times—to Seneca's chagrin—no aristocratic household was without a live-in dancing master to teach the newest movements and gestures to members of the family; and mime, an important part of classical dance, came out of a practical development during the Roman conquests—it was the best way for soldiers to get their orders across to conquered peoples of tongues not their own. What we call ballet, though, actually hatched in fifteenth-century Italy and matured in seventeenth- and eighteenth-century France, under the aegis of Louis XIV.

For many years before Louis, Italian troubadors strolled throughout Europe, singing and dancing and juggling. Catherine de Medici brought dancing Italian-style to France when she became that country's queen in 1573. She gave lavish fêtes and entertained French nobility with the court dances favored in Florence. By 1632, the performances were opened up to the public, and delight in dance spread beyond the castle walls.

Catherine was ballet's midwife, but Louis XIV was its guardian, its nurturer, its loving, adoptive parent. It was Louis who raised the art to just that, an art, and to a maturity that is still valid today. Louis's reign was a long one, from

1643 to 1715. During that time ballet blossomed, expanded, spread its delicate wings. Since then, through dancers, choreographers, and composers, classical dance has continued to evolve; its possibilities have increased and its horizons broadened dramatically, but ballet's basics were established in seventeenth-century France.

From Louis to Max, a line tracing ballet's development could be drawn in fewer than a dozen steps. It's astonishing how small the world of ballet is. Any history of classical dance puts one in mind of the calypso song "I'm My Own Grandpa," as everyone is related by blood or by marriage or by dance philosophy. The classical dance family now reaches around the world, with distant cousins recognizing one another at first glimpse. The great-great-great-great-great grandfather of them all was Louis XIV.

As a young man, Louis himself loved to dance. So, naturally, did all the men in his court—or at least they pretended to love to dance. If the king danced, the king's courtiers danced.

Soon, though, Louis's overindulgence in life's other pleasures took its toll, and the Sun King (whose nickname actually comes from a part he took in a dance, complete with heavy political overtones, of course) became too corpulent to cavort around the floor. Nevertheless, his interest in the lively art remained as avid as his other appetites, and he became dance's devoted royal patron.

In 1661, Louis established the first academy of dance. It was composed of thirteen masters who were supposed to codify the steps, establish standards, and teach the courtiers, who would then perform for the king's amusement. There is some debate as to just how much the dancing masters actually accomplished, but certainly the five positions and a number of steps were set down at the time, and French became the language not only of food and cooking but also of dance and dancing. To this day ballet students learn at least some of the language as they practice steps such as brissées, cabrioles, and entrechats, and as turns become tours and tendus are executed en terre and en l'air.

The dances of Louis's times were a lot easier than the ballets of today. Based on ancient folk dances, they consisted of quite simple marches and steps, and, like a football game halftime show, the forming and reforming of geometric patterns. All the dancers were men. For the most difficult sections a master was brought in. He was the expert, and he practiced a great deal more than the courtiers.

In Louis's court there were at least three masters who showed exceptional ability, but one, Pierre Beauchamp, really changed the face of ballet forever. Beauchamp was the first to go airborne, to make a full 360-degree turn while aloft, to establish the tour en l'air as a staple of the danseur's tricks. His ability to soar and spin had never been seen before and was unequaled by any of the other masters or dancing courtiers. By Beauchamp's time, the courtiers were losing interest in dancing, anyhow, and their skills were slipping. Dancing was hard work, and it took a lot of their time; and besides, the king wasn't rehearsing and performing anymore. Favor couldn't be curried as easily by dancing, so interest slacked, and the desire grew fainter and fainter. Then came Beauchamp, who was so damn good. Courtiers danced for position and status, and they were not about to compete with one who danced for pay. So they stopped trying and joined the audience. Thus was the professional danseur born.

As the pros took over, ability and dedication increased dramatically, and the teaching of dance became more and more important. It is always through the dancers-turned-teachers that this thing we call ballet is passed down through the generations. When the Russian Alexandra Danilova insists in America that her students do an arabesque on the diagonal because that is the French way to do it, she is reaching back through history, all the way back to the court of Louis XIV.

Another of Louis's dancing masters forged the first link in a still strong chain of great teaching. Louis DuPré, Le Grand DuPré. If Beauchamp was the Baryshnikov of his era, an exploding firecracker of a dancer, then DuPré was the Peter Martins. Tall, elegant, and princely, DuPré was the best example of his time of the *danseur noble*, the leading man of ballet, the one who always wins the ballerina. DuPré enthralled Parisian audiences, and he also traveled to London, where he danced with and for John Weaver, the founding father of British ballet. DuPré also established himself as number one among the Parisian ballet masters and counted among his pupils two pivotal evolutionary forces: Gaetan Vestris, the patriarch of the dancing dynasty; and Jean-Louis Noverre, the ballet reformer whose *Fifteen Letters on the Dance*, published in 1760—just sixteen years before America threw out the British and twenty-nine before the French overthrew the monarchy—revolutionized classical dance.

For his part, John Weaver did some incredible things in England. He danced and he taught and he choreographed, of course, but he did more than that. Before Weaver, ballet was always a part of the opera; in Paris, to this day, the most important company is the Paris Opera Ballet. Now, of course, the dancers perform without the singers, but back then, ballet was not separate from opera and was always accompanied by words—words sung and words spoken. Weaver choreo-

History repeats itself daily in SAB's Intermediate class.

Sherrie Nickol

graphed the first ballet that had no words at all, no actor explaining the plot, and no songs; Weaver banished words from dance. He enabled ballet to stand alone. He was not opposed to language, however, and he used words liberally himself. He wrote polemics about the importance to dance of music and gesture, emphasizing a new and sophisticated musicality in dancers, and he translated into English the major French text on ballet technique. The book was taken immediately to heart and classroom by all the ballet masters in London, and soon British ballet was taught the French way. Thus a commonality of purpose and effort was forged between the French and English, and the ballet family tree established a British branch that would strongly resemble its French relatives.

Weaver had a keen analytical mind; he took apart and wrote about the components of dance movement, just what went into these steps and combinations of steps, and he was the first ever to write about dancers' anatomy, to try to understand how a dancer's physical makeup—his bones and muscles—contributed to his ability to do the steps.

The English actor John Garrick called Jean-Louis Noverre the Shakespeare of Dance; still, Noverre had a terrible time getting people to listen to him, particularly in France. So he went to Germany and first published his treatise on balletic reform in Stuttgart, only later finding a home for his writings in his native land. With his *Letters*, Noverre sent out a call to arms; he demanded a drastic overhaul of classical dance, and he set down some very basic principles that are still followed carefully today. The elaborate plots then in vogue were simplified by Noverre, made much more down-to-earth and understandable, and he demanded the same paring down of ballet steps, as well, clarifying them and purging them of elaborate decoration.

Noverre insisted that dancers could not be just clever automatons, that drama and emotion and artistry were very, very important to dancing properly, and he got rid of all the intricate masks and headgear that were commonly used. He gave performers no place to hide; he exposed them and their faces. Dancers had to work harder now and do every step cleanly and clearly; no rococo combinations permitted blurred transitions. They also had to give up grimacing and gritting their teeth—no grunting and groaning. Their faces were in clear view, and now they had to make it look as though they were enjoying what they were doing. They had to smile; they had to breathe less visibly and less audibly. Just as more and more effort was being asked of them, they had to devise ways of letting the effort show less and less. They had to make it look easy, smooth, fluid. There is no other physical pursuit in which the perpetrators are not permitted to betray how they feel and how hard it all is. Dancers may collapse offstage and fall to the floor in agonized gasps to fill their lungs, but onstage they must look calm and beautiful.

A song from *A Chorus Line* says that "Everything was beautiful at the ballet." It's true; at least that's the aim, even though the physical demands often outpace those of huffing and puffing Olympic athletes or tennis players who emit loud noises with every connection of ball and racquet. We can thank Jean-Louis Noverre for adding that extra bit of beauty to the performance of ballet—as well as for many other early changes that we enjoy today.

We can also thank Noverre for becoming another link in that sturdy chain of great teaching. His pupils carried his work beyond what he was able to do, and one, Jean Dauberval, choreographed an example of the new, more natural style of dance that is still danced today. *La Fille Mal Gardée* is a simple love story about two young country folk. Of course, the ballet has been changed and changed from its earliest choreography, so that what we see today is quite different from the original, but it is still a simple story of simple young people who are just clever enough to outwit the powerful adults who try to stifle them. It seems fitting that the debut of this ballet was in 1789, the year of the French Revolution.

Until the end of the seventeenth century women didn't dance professionally in France. Performing for pay was not considered an appropriate behavior for a lady. Also, the women wouldn't have stood a chance. Their long skirts and many petticoats would have made complicated steps almost impossible to do, and their feet all but invisible.

But, by the 1680s, a few "ballerinas" had joined danseurs up on the stage, though they were still no competition for the men. Their movements were delicate and sweet, and what audiences wanted to see was the high leaping and fast spinning of the men. Soon the women would catch on, though, and start to catch up. Skirts would be shortened; costumes would be simplified. It was very shocking at first, but feet and ankles would emerge from under all that fabric and free up their owners to move better and faster and be seen more. For the remainder of the eighteenth century, though, men would continue to dominate classical dance.

By the end of Louis's reign, ballet was everywhere—Austria, Italy, Denmark, and Russia—but France remained dance's world capital and Paris its very heart and soul. All who were able came to Paris to study with the famous masters, like the family Vestris, Gaetan and his descendants.

Vestris *père* was a true character. A student of Le Grand DuPré, Gaetan was cast in his teacher's image—tall, elegant, noble. He was also conceited and self-absorbed beyond belief. He was born in 1729, and he entered the Paris Opera School in 1748, along with a sister and a brother. The Vestrises were descended from Italian troubadors who had settled in France after wandering the Continent; you might call the clan an early version of a show-business family. Gaetan enjoyed continuous acclaim as a dancer, and he and his son Auguste were regarded as absolute paragons, appearing together throughout Europe in halls filled to overflowing with enthusiastic fans. No one thought more highly of his own abilities than Gaetan, however, who once turned with horror to a woman who had stepped on his toe on a Parisian boulevard and said, "My dear madame, you have put all of Paris into mourning for two weeks."

Tales of Gaetan's extravagant behavior are many. A favorite is the one about his argument with the Paris Opera's ballet master, which resulted in the dancer's brandishing a sword. That little incident landed Vestris in jail, but he was completely undaunted. While there, he lived in lavish quarters and entertained his friends in grand style, hosting sumptuous dinner parties every week. Once, years later, his son Auguste was threatened with the possibility of incarceration, and the father recommended it as an extremely pleasant interlude.

Auguste was a better dancer than even his father. This Gaetan minded not at all, as it reflected well on his own teaching. Also, when the father and son danced together, the excitement doubled. It is said that for one of their performances in London, Parliament adjourned so its members could see the duo. Each Vestris was known as Le Dieu de la Danse, but the father may have chosen the appellation for himself. Gaetan was not above suggesting that his students might want to kiss his foot, and he was also convinced that his century had produced but three great men: Voltaire, Frederick the Great of Prussia—and himself.

Auguste had a dancing style that was very different from his father's. He was an extremely high jumper; he seemed to hover in the air like a hummingbird. Watching him once, a woman exclaimed to her companion, "He must live on a diet of butterflies," only to be told, "No, my dear, he just eats the wings." Auguste was the finest dancer Paris had ever seen, and the finest they would see for a very long time—until 1908, in fact, and Nijinsky. Both Auguste and his father danced and taught until well past middle age, but the son was not able to top his father in longevity. Gaetan made his last appearance on stage in 1800, at the age of seventy-one, on the occasion of his fourth grandson's debut with the Paris Opera. He died eight years later. Auguste's last appearance was in 1835, when he danced a minuet with Marie Taglioni, she who was to sound the death knell for the danseur and send him to oblivion.

Auguste did take precedence over his father in ballet's history, however, both as a dancer and a teacher. In 1969, preparing for an important ballet contest in Moscow, the young Mikhail Baryshnikov learned a new ballet that had been made especially for him to wow the judges. The work was called *Vestris*, and it brought back to life the daring leaps of Auguste. Misha was more than up to the task, and he won the gold medal. Ballerina Maya Plisetskaya was one of the judges. She said that the young Baryshnikov deserved "thirteen points out of a possible twelve."

Early on, French ballet established a strong grip on the Russian imagination. Peter the Great, who was hell-bent on westernizing and Frenchifying his country, brought in French danseurs to perform and demonstrate. Then, in 1734, the Empress Anna imported a French dancing master to teach the delicate and gentle airs of court dancing to her French-speaking entourage, and by 1738, a school of ballet had been established in the attic of the Winter Palace, its students twelve cadets from the Imperial naval academy and twelve girls from among the staff of the palace. The school, of course, became the Imperial School, the academy that trained Georgi Balanchivadze and Vaslav Nijinsky. Later it was renamed the Vaganora Choreographic Institute, where Mikhail Baryshnikov and Rudolf Nureyev both learned their craft.

The French influence endured in Russia (although that first master was followed by an Austrian and an Italian and later a Swede), but local folk dances and Russian enthusiasm, ebullience, and energy also influenced choreographers and ballet masters to create livelier, gutsier works. When the Romantic Era took over Europe and elevated the ballerina to such heights that the danseur was forgotten, the Russian male managed to avoid being taken over completely. He was downplayed but not lost.

In Denmark dance had enjoyed royal patronage for centuries, but little development in ballet took place until a French family named Bournonville appeared in Copenhagen. And it was almost an accident, or an act of fate, that this name, which is now synonymous with Danish ballet and with great male dancing, took root in Copenhagen. Antoine Bournonville, father of the great choreographer August, was a contemporary and friend of Auguste Vestris; if the elder Bournonville had stayed in his native France, it is said, he just might have given the last Dieu de la Danse a jeté for his money at the title. But Antoine was invited by King Gustavus III of Sweden to come to Stockholm and enliven the ballet there; it was an offer he could not and did not refuse. When the king was assassinated in 1792, Antoine headed home to France but stopped in Copenhagen to visit a former pupil. While there, he performed with the Royal Danes to rave reviews, and he also fell quickly, desperately, deeply in love. He could not bear to leave his new sweetheart, so he abandoned thoughts of Paris, married her, and settled in Copenhagen.

August received his first training with his father but was eventually able to convince the king of Denmark that it would be a good investment to send him to Paris to learn all the latest developments in dance. He stayed in the French capital for five years, trained under Auguste Vestris, and returned home just in time to save the local ballet from near extinction and to become one of the most important names in the history of classical dance.

Bournonville style and Bournonville ballets are the hallmarks of the current Royal Danish company and were, all during the Romantic Era, the only truly safe harbor for the danseur. For it was August Bournonville, and only he, who ignored the total reverence for the ballerina, who refused to abandon the male to a life of just lifting the female star, who redefined the roles of male and female in dance, and who demanded strong and sprightly leaps and leg beats from both boys and girls.

It was a close call. All European hearts were yearning for Romantic values—in music, in poetry, and in dance. Classicism was out of vogue; the cycle was turning. And then a young Italian ballerina debuted in a work choreographed for her by her father.

The year was 1832, the ballerina Marie Taglioni, the ballet *La Sylphide*. There had been "toe dancing" before Taglioni; there had been lifts by partners to make ballerinas look as though they were sailing through the air. But both were few and far between, and they hadn't interfered with the male proprietorship of the airspace above the floor, which only men were strong enough to leap up to and through. Suddenly the altitudes were no longer private property. There was Taglioni, high atop hard pointe shoes, about to take flight, then covering the floor in tiny steps on her toes (bourées), looking as though she were floating across the floor. And at the end, with the aid of machinery, she did fly off the stage.

Audiences swooned. No one had seen such sublime

110

and ethereal grace. No one had even believed it possible. Taglioni was the essence of romanticism, of delicate femininity, of wafting idealism. There was no turning back. The ballerina was in ascendance, and the danseur in her shadow. Soon writers would wax eloquent over the charms of Marie, of Elssler, of Cerutto and Grissi. Some even expressed repulsion and dismay over the idea of maleness, of heavy muscles and taut necks in dance.

The situation became further aggravated and exaggerated by greedy impresarios eager to highlight the charms of their beautiful girls and downplay the strengths of their male counterparts; the women themselves were not averse to hogging the spotlight, either. That sweet, ethereal Marie Taglioni kept her partner, Jules Perrot, from dancing with her at *Sylphide*'s premiere because she didn't want any competition from him; he was too popular for her taste, and she wanted all eyes on herself. She eventually even managed to get him banned from the Paris Opera altogether. Clearly, baroque politics continued long after Louis's court; ballet is still a world rife with intrigue and emotion and plots against competitors.

In America, the San Francisco Ballet is just recovering from the madness accompanying a change of directors. Everyone, including local press, took sides vehemently, and eventually security guards were posted backstage to keep the ousted chief from appearing onstage for bows every time one of his works was performed. Delicate, sweet ballerinas go after each other, too, and more than one upcoming star has told of finding bits of glass in her toe shoes just before an important debut. In Taglioni's time the women were not fighting each other yet; their campaign was to steal the thunder away from the men. And steal it they did.

Choreographers began to concentrate exclusively on

the ballerinas and their newfound airiness, and choice parts for men soon became fewer and fewer. Naturally, so did choice men. Why would the best bother to pursue ballet when there was nothing to attract them? In some situations danseurs were dispensed with altogether, and women were dressed up *en travestie* to do their parts—all but the heavy lifting, that is. A few big lugs were always kept on staff to come out to hoist and carry. It was the era of the danseur as *porteur,* as hauling machine, as crane. By the end of the nineteenth century in Europe, the danseur had been all but banished from the stage.

Meanwhile, in America, opinions about dance differed. Confusion was the order of the day. In the more elite of the colonies, such as Virginia, ballroom dancing enjoyed great favor. Minuets were the rage, along with powdered wigs, fancy gowns, and gentle turns around the parquet. In those early days there was even a professional dancer, the first on record. His name was John Durang, and he had a long, happy career. He even danced for George Washington, who was himself an active and enthusiastic social dancer. Durang could hardly have been called a ballet dancer, however. His specialties were the jig and the hornpipe, two styles of dance much more suited to rugged Americans. There was little precedent here for the aristocratic, courtly manners of ballet; America needed a more open, energetic kind of dance. John Durang supplied it.

The Puritans had a large impact on the development, or the delay in development, of ballet in the United States. Those stringent folks were always in conflict as to how they felt about dancing. The Bible approved of it, they knew, but still, it seemed too much, too dangerous. They knew absolutely that men and women should never dance together; that was clear, and they were also confident that moving one's body around in front of others for pay—dancing professionally—was a giant step in the direction of sin, degradation, and eternal damnation. Add to their number the large group of folks who wanted to rid the States of any and all European influences and devise new democratic, all-American pursuits, and you have the basis for a strong prejudice against classical dance. The decline of the danseur in Europe tipped the balance. The insistence that men who danced ballet were nothing more than effeminate misfits took deep root in this country, deeper even than at its source.

Amazingly, in spite of all the odds against it, early nineteenth-century America did produce one fine, home-grown danseur. His name was George Washington Smith, and he was a tall, handsome Philadelphian. Smith made his performing debut in 1832; he started off dancing the clogs and hornpipes that were so popular, but he went on from there to classical dance. His first opportunity to study ballet seriously came in 1841, when the famous European ballerina Fanny Elssler came to America on tour and stayed for two years. Traveling with her was her ballet master, the elegantly named Louis Sylvain, who had actually been born in Ireland with the more simple moniker of Sullivan. Smith danced with Elssler and studied with Sylvain. He learned steps and gestures and mime, and he turned into a fine, bravura danseur and a definitive Harlequin, the commedia dell'arte character still danced today.

Smith soon had the American franchise on male classical dance; he was all there was, and he worked constantly—enough to install his beautiful young wife in a huge house in Philadelphia and to father ten children with her. Smith danced with everyone—all the American ballerinas of the time and all the visitors on tour, including the infamous Lola Montez. Smith and Mary Ann Lee danced the first all-American *Giselle,* and he appeared regularly with another U.S. dancer, Julia Trumbull. During one of his guest-squiring stints Miss Trumbull became so enraged and jealous of the Italian ballerina he was partnering that she stormed the theater and churned up the audience so that the two couldn't come out and dance. A riot actually broke out, and it took police to remove the jealous Julia, restore calm, and permit the show to go on.

Smith made it to Paris to study at the Opera, and he also danced in Italy. No stranger to jealousy, Smith insisted that his wife keep the curtains drawn in the parlor of their Stateside home while he was away so she could not gaze out into the street and be tempted by some passing gentleman. Only one of the Smith progeny turned to dance, a boy named Joseph, and he later wrote that his ever-so-masculine father had enough ability to master triple tours en l'air (tough to this day) and that once, when his dad was having a hard time with entrechat quatres, he practiced them hard and long enough to double their number and add huits to his repertory.

By the time Smith died, in 1899, male dancing had reached its nadir, and the future for danseurs looked bleak indeed. But hope was on its way, even though no one knew it. A few months before Smith's death, a young Polish boy was accepted at Russia's Imperial School. He seemed a wonder of natural dance ability and perfect facility. His name was Vaslav Nijinsky. The minute he entered the Imperial School, young Vaslav became privy to the most complete and advanced balletic knowledge of the time. Paris had petered out; St. Petersburg had become the new ballet world capital. The Bournonville-trained Christian Johansson, who had been training Russian dancers for decades, was still teaching, though in his eighties. The Italian master, Enrico Cecchetti, had been imported to Russia as well, and the Frenchman Marius Petipa was the man in charge. Nijinsky learned the very best of French, Danish, and Italian ballet, all combined with Russian heart and soul.

Word got around fast, and soon Nijinsky was a prized and cosseted student. At the time a young, frustrated chore-ographer named Mikhail Fokine was searching for new, un Petipa-like ways to express himself in dance. As if in answer to his prayer, an American woman who had all Europe eating out of her decidedly unclassical hand made a tour of Russia. In her bare feet and clad in just a few wisps of chiffon, Isadora Duncan astounded the Russians with her "natural" dances and made Fokine feel as though he had been freed from bondage. She became his inspiration, and Vaslav Nijinsky became his instrument.

Fokine and Nijinsky joined up with the tyrannical avant-garde impresario Serge Diaghilev and set off for Paris. Together the triumvirate gave new life to the male dancer; together they reinstalled him in a place of prominence on the ballet stage. In 1909, Paris saw Nijinsky for the first time, in a full evening of Russian ballet that had been eagerly awaited. It was the height of the season in the capital, and everyone was there. In a solo designed by Fokine to show off his virtuosity, Nijinsky stunned the audience into a moment of speechlessness. Then roaring applause drowned out all at-tempts at conversation. Not since the great Auguste Vestris had French dance lovers seen such power and artistry, such control and total delight in movement.

The world would be blessed with Nijinsky's gifts only for a decade, ten years during which Fokine would make three of the greatest ballets for men on him—*Spectre de la Rose, Petrouchka,* and *Scheherazade*—but he has ever since been the standard against which all male dancing is measured. The rest of Diaghilev's company had to take a clear second place to the star, a situation that so unnerved his famous partner Anna Pavlova that she left the Ballets Russes and struck off on her own, touring widely in a small company with small-scale works that showcased only her. Nijinsky's turbulent relationship with Diaghilev and his tormented end have been exhaustively documented, most interestingly in Richard Buckle's biography, *Nijinsky.* In that book Buckle sums up the dancer's life as, ". . . ten years growing, ten years learning, ten years dancing, thirty years in eclipse. . . . Roughly sixty in all." Nijinsky died in 1950, in England; three years later Serge Lifar had his body exhumed and reburied in Montmartre, next to Auguste Vestris. During his brief, blazing career Nijinsky made only one American tour, but his former partner Pavlova traveled the States from coast to coast like a pioneer, bringing ballet to big cities and small towns alike. Dropouts from her troupe took on vital roles in American dance—Adolph Bolm taught in Chicago and ran the San Francisco Opera Ballet for a time, and Michael Mordkin danced in New York and founded a company there that would be the predecessor of American Ballet Theatre.

Fokine also settled in New York and became a most important teacher. Among his students were Willam Christiansen, the eldest member of a trio of brothers who became responsible for any serious ballet west of the Great Divide, and the youthful Lincoln Kirstein.

When Kirstein and Balanchine opened the doors of the School of American Ballet in 1934, they weren't really sure what to expect. They did know that they would have all adult students at first, as they had gathered most of them—some say raided—from Catherine Littlefield's school in Philadelphia. They also knew that they would have Dorothie Littlefield as a teacher for the beginners; that was part of the bargain.

They had no clue, however, that fortune would be so generous as to deliver to them a gift from the heart of America—the Christiansen brothers, Lew and Harold—and they didn't even learn until later that there was yet another Christiansen, Willam. The brothers hailed from Brigham City, Utah. They were handsome, manly, and able. Their Danish grandfather, Lars, had settled in the States, converted to Mormonism, and become the patriarch of a huge, polygamous family. Lars was a dancer and fiddler who taught his young grandsons his native folk dances. Their Uncle Pete—L. P. Christiansen—gave his nephews their first ballet training. "I won't say he was highly professional," says Willam, "but he was better than anyone else." What Uncle Pete taught the boys was ballet Italian-style. He and his two brothers had studied with Stefano Mascagno, a contemporary of Cecchetti's, and so he filled the little Christiansens with Milanese technique, mixed with American enthusiasm and a dash of Danish delicacy for good measure.

The second generation of Christiansens established schools throughout the western states of Idaho, Washington, and Oregon, offering their Mascagno Method, and they dramatically raised the level of consciousness and of training west of Chicago. Uncle Frederick danced and played cello with the Seattle Symphony; a student of his was Merce Cunningham, the pioneer modern dancer. Uncle Moses started the symphony orchestra in Portland.

Willam, Lew, and Harold's father, Christian B. Christiansen, was a conductor who put together an act for his boys and took them on the road. Le Crist Review featured a quartet of dancers, at first consisting of Willam, Lew, and two girls (Harold was at West Point at the time), with dad leading the musicians. Comments Willam, "We were in this thing before we had enough sense to stay out of it." The name of the group changed several times, to the Four Spirals, then the Mascagno Four, then Christiansen Bros. & Co., and finally to simply the Christiansen Brothers. The foursome pirouetted all along that great American trail—vaudeville: Los Angeles, Chicago, New York, and just about every whistle-stop in between witnessed the Christiansens' "interpretive, expressive" dancing. What they saw was a boiled-down version of ballet, liberally laced with to-the-ceiling jumps and multiple turns aloft delivered "faster than airmail." Dressed in dramatic, open-necked black shirts with billowy sleeves, black pants, and vivid cummerbunds, the boys raised their partners on high as though they were offering a toast with glasses of vintage champagne. Their glamorous ladies were clad in glitzy costumes of silk and chiffon, adorned with sequins and beads. They had tutus made completely of peacock feathers, and their feet were enveloped in satin slippers with hard, stiff toes. Boiled-down or not, it was ballet they were dancing, and the girls went up *en pointe* just like Marie Taglioni or Anna Pavlova. Though the boys occasionally donned dramatic capes for swirling and affixed satin hats to their heads and glittering masks to their noses, they never, ever pulled ballet dancer's tights up on over their legs. "If we'd ever appeared in tights," says Willam, "they'd have booed us off the stage."

Along their way on tours of the circuit, this jolly band of classy semi-classicists shared bills with W. C. Fields and Jack Benny, among others, and they even played the Palace. Says Willam, "The general audience had no idea of what we were doing. . . . There were times we weren't even sure what the hell we were. We studied with all the good teachers in every city we hit—Albertieri, Bolm, Fokine—but some things we learned by chance. You know those soft landings that are so hard to teach the boys how to do when they jump, keeping the heels off the floor until the last minute and remembering to plié? Well, we had to learn how to do that out of necessity. We always warmed up backstage, while other acts were on, so we couldn't make any noise. We had to figure out a way to jump quietly so we wouldn't interfere with what was going on. We didn't know that we were learning the right way; no one had told us; we just knew what we had to do."

Willam moved to Portland, Oregon, in 1931 with his ailing wife (she was a native Portlander who had trained there in the Christiansen-family-owned ballet school before becoming Willam's partner in the act and then in life), and Harold dropped out of the military academy and into the quartet. Soon vaudeville fell into decline, as movies got more and more technically able and captured more and more of the public's imagination. Not so gradually, moving pictures sneaked their way into the great old vaudeville houses, and soon theater after theater closed its stage to live performers and opened its cash registers to the profits brought in by filmed musical extravaganzas. In order to stay solvent, Lew, Harold, and their partners joined the huge cast of an operetta called *The Great Waltz*, which was being performed in New York's Rockefeller Center. They hated it, but they had to do something. While in *Waltz*, the boys decided to go over and take some classes from a Russian named Balanchine. Another chapter in ballet history was about to begin, and America was about to start her rise to dominance in the world of classical dance.

Lew was the most gifted dancer of the Christiansens;

he embodied all the American attributes that Balanchine was eager to capitalize on: strength, speed, athleticism. He had a wonderful ballet body and high energy, all held together by a gentle, fresh, and trusting spirit. Lew became the first American to dance Balanchine's *Apollo*, his seminal work, to music by Stravinsky, which had been choreographed on Serge Lifar. In *Thirty Years/The New York City Ballet*, Lincoln Kirstein wrote, "[Lew] danced the best [*Apollo*] both Balanchine and I have ever seen. . . . He combined in one body beauty, perfect physical endowment, musicality of a high professional level, a developed acrobatic technique and an elegance of stage manners which was an exact reflection of his inherent morality. Also, he would prove to be a dancer of taste, ingenuity, and humor." After Stravinsky saw Lew Christiansen dance the part of the young god to his music, the composer went backstage to offer his thanks to the dancer.

If George Washington Smith was America's first premier danseur, then Lew Christiansen was our second, and many years separated the two. Nothing much was going on for American danseurs in the interim, but a proud and lively heritage of tap dancing became part of our style and psyche. Not too many Americans know who Lew Christiansen was, but Gene Kelly is surely a household name, and the name Fred Astaire brings a smile to the lips of several generations of contented moviegoers. Astaire and Kelly made tap dancing an acceptable activity for young American boys—could ballet then be far behind? Many, many males pirouetting today came to ballet through the back door: tap. Choreographer Michael Smuin is one of them. When he was growing up in Montana, he decided he just *had* to be like Gene Kelly. The works he creates today are almost theatrical enough for his idol to star in them. Richard Rapp was also a tap dancer first and a ballet dancer second, and it took him ten lessons at the barre to admit he was studying ballet and to discard his slacks for tights.

The Kaiser brothers are a whole family of ballet dancers whose toes tapped long before they pointed. The eldest is Roy. When he was but four and a decidedly physical kid, Roy's mother enrolled him in her friend's tap-dancing class as an alternative to preschool and as a safety valve for her own sanity. The Kaisers were not a show business family; Roy's father is a businessman who now works for a lumber company in Seattle. There was no thought of wanting Roy to take dance seriously, to become a pro; they just wanted him to use up some of his excess energy and enjoy a good time.

Mauck Studio

Four of the five tap-dancing Kaiser brothers are now professional ballet dancers.

He loved the lessons, and soon his younger brother Kevin started tapping too. Then Danny followed, Kenny, and finally Russell.

The Dancing Kaisers were born. Soon they had tapped their way into hearts, homes, and school auditoriums all around their home base. "It was great fun," says Roy, "because it got us out of school regularly and earned us some money too."

Roy never had any interest in ballet whatever. "I thought it was only for sissies," he says. When he was seventeen, though, he took a class one day on a whim—dressed in Levi's. Something clicked, and "I just decided to pursue it," he says, adding that it took *him* several more classes before he had the courage to leave his jeans behind and pull on some tights. Many good old American boys who don't mind one bit appearing in the skintight bottoms of football uniforms, or in itsy-bitsy track shorts or the teeny-weeny swim-racer's bikini uniform recoil in horror from the ballet dancer's required tights. In fact, an entry should be made in the encyclopedia of psychological disorders—Danskinophobia: extreme fear of wearing tights. The disease used to be rampant; the epidemic is over now, but isolated cases still crop up.

Roy managed to conquer his anxiety and become a fine and elegant dancer, and soon his younger brothers joined him at the barre, one at a time. Now four of the five are professional ballet dancers. Roy and Danny Kaiser are both with the Pennsylvania Ballet, Kevin dances in Seattle with Pacific Northwest, and Russell is in the NYCB.

Until quite recently, most Americans agreed with Roy that ballet was only for sissies, skinny sisters, or maybe Kelly and Astaire. American boys were traditionally encouraged to

Roy, the oldest Kaiser, at his first ballet class. Note the Levi's.

play at sports and work at becoming President, or doctor or general or hero—or at least a fireman—but not some pansy in tights. Dance was thought to be a refuge for those who weren't smart enough to do anything else, or those who wanted to be as much like women as they could, and no American parents wanted their sons to be considered effeminate or dumb or both. And besides, dancers could never earn a decent living. Ballet was okay for a beautiful daughter. Beautiful daughters weren't supposed to go out and make money and be independent; also, there is always a cadre of wealthy doctors, lawyers, and corporate chiefs dying to marry beautiful ballerina daughters. Sons, on the other hand, were supposed to become the doctors, lawyers, and corporate chiefs who married ballerinas. Sons were supposed to get on about making something of themselves, doing "something serious," begetting families and providing for them. Well, the times have finally changed. At last daughters are permitted to become investment bankers if they want to, and sons are permitted to dance. Prejudice against dancing for American men is definitely on the wane; the ghost of Marie Taglioni is finally being put to rest.

Education and exposure to ballet have done the trick. Tours throughout the land started the process. Balanchine and SAB legitimized the training and upgraded performance levels. The Ford Foundation supplied a lot of money, and movies and television increased exponentially the numbers of Americans eager for the next pas de deux. Millions of Americans now appreciate classical dance. Attendance at live performances rises yearly, and those who can't get to a theater can often see top-notch dancing in the safety of their own living rooms. Says Michael Smuin, "TV brings ballet to places like Buzzard's Breath, Wyoming, and every year technical breakthroughs improve the way dance is photographed for television, so that the home viewer sees more and sees better. Back in '78, my *Romeo and Juliet* had four performances on *Dance in America*. Forty million people watched it. If the San Francisco Ballet played to a full house every night of the year, it would take 35.2 years to reach 40 million people."

The electronic miracle has enabled many, many Americans to see for themselves that danseurs are not necessarily what they thought, that they are courageous, strong, handsome, serious, and committed, that what they are doing is interesting, valuable, even dangerous, and that they obviously love doing it. TV isn't the whole story, though. American men have had some valuable help from their friends across oceans and continents in establishing themselves on their own turf and on their own terms. Balanchine, Baryshnikov, Nureyev, Martins . . . none was born here; all have played a huge role in getting ballet for men accepted on these shores.

In 1961, Rudolf Nureyev became front-page news when he left the Soviet Union forever while on tour with the Kirov in Paris. Americans were soon captivated by his story, his amazing Tartar cheekbones, and a soaring jump that sent shivers down the spines of all who were lucky enough to trace its arc with naked or binoculared eyes. Nureyev always dressed and lived with a flair as breathtaking as his onstage moves, and he brought a glamour, excitement, and mystery to the role of danseur that no American would have been permitted. In fact, we had two all-American danseurs at the time who were working hard and well to improve the image of the dancing male. Jacques d'Amboise and Edward Villella danced for George Balanchine onstage; they danced for Ed Sullivan on television; they were in movies and featured in *Life* magazine, and they were inspiring many Americans to have more respect for dancers and for dancing. Still, it required someone with Nureyev's exotic background, dramatic defection, and overwhelming style to skyrocket male dancers into the same category as movie stars and pop singers.

X.

Pioneers

School of American Ballet teacher Suki Shorer feels that the 1977 movie *The Turning Point* was the real turning point in American attitudes toward men dancing. "Remember," says Shorer, "it's the mothers who have to be convinced, and seeing Misha in that movie did it for many of them. The movie allowed women who had never seen Eddie or Jacques to say, 'I want my son to be like that. That's okay for my son.' "

Baryshnikov has certainly done his part—in *The Turning Point*, in *White Nights*, onstage and on television. He is arguably the finest dancer the world has ever seen, and he can do any kind of dance. He leaps like Vestris, partners like a prince, and knocks off modern, tap, and Broadway routines with ease. He is also sexy, adorable, and determinedly heterosexual. Boys want to be like him, and mothers fantasize about being with him. There is no question about what he's done for the image of the male dancer, and now there is no question about how American he is, either. Remember the Statue of Liberty Centennial celebration? That's when Misha became a citizen of his adopted land. Still, even with his once-in-a-long-time combination of ability and appeal, even

Baryshnikov could not have done what he's done if others hadn't prepared the way. *The Turning Point* did not spring full-grown from his powerful thighs. The groundwork, the spading and the hoeing, had been going on for years.

Says Peter Martins, "Balanchine knew it would take a long time. Jacques and Eddie opened up people's eyes. Then the Russian defectors brought a certain glamour and made male dancing fashionable to look at. The *Dance in America* television series had a real impact, and then there are all the rest of us . . . who knew it would be better to do it the real way, by trying for excellence and waiting until people recognized it. I'm glad Mr. B. lived long enough to see the blossoms from the seeds he planted."

Show-business families always understood about the fun men who dance have, and ballet fathers have often begat dancing sons—starting with the Vestrises, Bournonvilles and Petipas, working through the years down to George Washington Smith and the Christiansens, then the d'Amboises and the Martinses.

In countries with state-supported ballet, families are honored when their sons are chosen to be members of the Royal Ballet or to become a People's Artist. In America it was always true that families a bit lower down the social totem pole were more pleased to find their boys interested in classical dance than families whose sons had greater expectations. Now that has changed. Sons of doctors, book editors, and business bigwigs are becoming ballet dancers, and their fathers are feeling perfectly free to admit it to their golfing chums. There is even a serious dance program now at St. Paul's Academy, a big-league, very traditional New England prep school in Concord, New Hampshire. Former ABT dancer Richard Rein is in charge of dance there. He teaches boys; he teaches girls; hockey players flock in for an elective, and one male student, Philip Neal, danced at the International Ballet Competition in Jackson, Mississippi. Rein plans for the program to turn out professional dancers. Neal will no doubt be his first.

Back in 1942, when eight-year-old Jackie Ahearn was brought to Balanchine by his mother, there were very few boys his age dancing. The Ahearns were simple people, and Jackie's mother wanted more for her son than what was available on the streets of their Washington Heights neighborhood. She wanted culture, grace, and elegance for her boy; she wanted him to have some of the finer accoutrements of life. So she gave him her maiden name, her romantic spirit, and an introduction to Mr. Balanchine. It turned out to be an arranged marriage that worked. Jacques d'Amboise may have taken a French name, but he turned out to be a classical dancer who could have come only from America. Tall, muscular, and with an openness as big as our Western plains and a boy-next-door grin, d'Amboise showed America the joy of dancing.

D'Amboise joined the City Ballet at the age of fifteen, and he danced with the company for more than three decades before retiring to run his National Dance Institute. He was in the 1950s movies *Carousel* and *Seven Brides for Seven Brothers*, and more than one *Life* magazine article featured him, generally in bathing trunks to show off his beautiful, strong body, and generally with his wife and babies around to attest to his fidelity and heterosexuality. The Ballet Dancer as All-American Boy. He was also a dancer with tremendous skill, grace, and crowd appeal, and his fans are legion. Long after age and abuse had taken a severe toll on his abilities and he was just doing a few not-too-taxing parts, audiences in New York's

State Theater would roar their affection the minute d'Amboise placed one gnarled and twisted foot on the stage. He danced for so long that more than one generation grew up with him; everyone thinks he knows Jacques d'Amboise, and that's a big help to Jacques and his Institute. People are more apt to donate to someone they know.

All the time he was dancing, Jacques was a fine role model and eloquent spokesman for the male dancer. Now he is fulfilling his Johnny-Appleseed-like dream of sowing the desire for dance among the fields of American school children. His Institute sets up programs in public schools—for boys. Girls can join if and when there is space, but not until all the interested boys have been signed up. D'Amboise doesn't teach the kids classical dance, but he does give them a few basics, and he gets them moving to music. Every year he also gives them a chance to perform by putting on a huge, star-studded show at Madison Square Garden's Felt Forum.

D'Amboise is a shimmering bundle of energy and a master at courting publicity. Everyone is interested in him. Films have been made on the Institute—with directors volunteering their services—television covers the Institute's activities, and newspapers regularly chart its progress and that of its founder. Jacques even managed to arrange a kind of quasi-cultural exchange between the Institute and China. He traveled to Beijing, spread his enthusiastic and cheerful brand of dance around to a passel of Chinese kids, and brought a bunch of them back here to perform for the cameras and at his super recital. For the annual show, known artists design the sets; musicians and singers perform for free; New York City policemen do a dance number in uniform; and New York City Ballet dancers show how the pros do it. One regular each year is Jacques's son Christopher, who has been known to squeeze rehearsals and performance for his dad between simultaneous obligations as a City Ballet principal dancer and as one of the stars of Broadway's *Song and Dance*. Energy runs in the family.

Comments Jacques d'Amboise of all his peripatetic efforts, "My life was transformed by the arts, and I never paid for a lesson, not dancing, not acting. I feel I have a debt, and I also have an ability and a need. Teaching ballet on a high level is really choreography. I like to choreograph for great dancers, but this is my idea of teaching."

Boys start ballet for a wide variety of reasons now. Some get inspired by one of the stars; some, like the Christiansens, are born into it. Some, like the Kaisers, just slide into it. Some are pushed by mothers who danced or who wished they had, and some start because they get bored waiting for their sisters to finish class, and it's better to dance than sit. In recent years more and more have come to classical dance through sport. For over a decade now, coaches on professional, college, and even high-school teams have used ballet exercises and simple steps to try to stretch out their often muscle-bound maulers and slam-dunkers, and to try to give them added agility and speed. Occasionally the athletes show a real flair for dance. Julius Erving, for instance, the beloved Doctor J., is as flexible and graceful as a ballet dancer, and he can hang in the air like Nijinsky, suspended over the basket just long enough to make you realize that he is doing the impossible. Former Pittsburgh Steeler Lynn Swann liked dancing so much, he continued classes on his own and is now on the board of directors of the Pittsburgh Ballet. Making a connection between ballet and sport has helped many Americans lose their fear of dance, helped them to see it as something different and glorious, not effete and precious. Says Suki Shorer, "The fact that so many athletes are using ballet has really made it easier for boys to start lessons. Americans just love athletes."

Max Fuqua was sent to ballet by sport. His gymnastics coach thought the boy could become a world-class competitor, Olympic material, and he wanted him to have an edge in an area where American gymnasts are usually not so strong—in the floor exercises, the most balletic part of any gymnastics routine. Little did the coach know that Max would like ballet better than gymnastics and that he would lose the most promising athlete he had come across in years. Max's chum Mark, the one who got into Special Men's at fourteen, thought ballet would enhance his hockey. Others want to be ahead of the competition on the soccer field or wrestling mat, but they, too, end up being enticed by Terpsichore's charms. Once in a while Max will muse, "If I had stayed with gymnastics, I'd be much farther ahead by now." Then he will quickly add, "But gymnastics hasn't got half the prestige that ballet has." Former SAB student Edwin Mota, who now dances professionally in Europe, says, "Ballet is everything. You have to be athletic and also artistic. In Mexico City, where I come from, some kids used to tease me about being a dancer. At first it bothered me, but after one year I would say to them, 'Can you do what I do?' "

The man most responsible for the turning of the training tables between dance and sport is Edward Villella. There's a bit of irony here, too, because Villella's mother brought him to SAB to get him away from sports. Eddie was a natural athlete, coordinated, strong, tough, and quick, and he competed constantly on the playing fields and in street games. One day he was beaned with a baseball and knocked unconscious. Mrs. Villella vowed that would never happen again; that was it, and she dragged young Eddie along to his sister's ballet class. The teachers at SAB took one look at the small, dark, muscular boy and signed him up immediately. He was ten years old. Jacques was only one year older, but he had already been at SAB for three years when Eddie arrived. The two are dancing opposites. Villella is dark, fiery, intense. Speed and power were his hallmarks. It was said of him that he came at the audience "like a fist" across the footlights. New York City Ballet dancer Larry Matthews says, "Eddie was like King Kong unleashed."

Villella's training was interrupted for four years when his father insisted that his son go to college to learn something that could get him a "real" job. His athletic conquests while at the New York Maritime College have filled his living room with boxing and baseball trophies, which sit on antique tables next to dance awards and an Emmy for a dance show. When Villella was performing, he was the most active campaigner for the male dancer as athlete. He set out to prove the strength and sports ability of dancers single-handedly, and basically he succeeded. He compared dancing to chasing a foul ball or going fifteen rounds in the boxing ring. He worked out with teams; he went on television regularly and talked about winning and losing in ballet. In 1969, *Life* asked whether Villella wasn't "The Country's Best Athlete," and in 1971, *Sports Illustrated* featured a long, admiring article about him.

Eddie Villella has done more for the male dancer than just prove he is athletic and not girlish, however. He has brought countless young men onto their feet, and he has tried his damnedest to prove that ballet dancers can earn a decent living. Determined that he would amass as much money as he possibly could, Villella constantly danced here, choreographed there, spoke someplace else. For years he lived a schedule that would have done in a less strong or less obsessed individual. He was hell-bent on proving that this honorable profession could earn a man enough to support a family or two (he has had two) and to buy all the material pleasures one could desire. When he talked in schools about dancing to skeptical tough boys whose first question was how much money he made, he always replied, "About as much as Tom Seaver."

Maybe if Villella hadn't been forced to take four years off from dance to go to college, maybe if his father had believed in ballet a bit more, then perhaps he might not have been so determined to prove that his is a good profession for a man. Maybe he had to prove it to his father as much as to anyone else. One thing is sure, though. Eddie Villella, who has been on presidential commissions, who has traveled the world because of dance, who had directed companies and is now in charge of a new troupe in Miami, who has a beautiful wife and two children and a Manhattan town house filled with antiques, that same Eddie Villella has never earned a single dime using the skills he learned at the Maritime College. Ballet has been responsible for all that he has, including his memories. Says he, "To have been part of the raw material for Balanchine's genius . . . that's mine for the rest of my life."

Lew Christiansen was still dancing with Balanchine when Jacques d'Amboise started in 1942, but by the time Villella arrived, Lew had been sent to Europe on tour—with the United States Army. The war years, the time Lew spent without ballet class, without dancing, without barre work, and without proper food, were disastrous to his technique; and when he came home, he found his former virtuosity was a thing of the past. He still danced, though; he took on somewhat less difficult parts, and he continued to choreograph (his work, *Filling Station*, had already been done, in 1938). He also took on a ballet mastership for Lincoln Kirstein.

Willam Christiansen, having started a professional ballet company while he was in Portland, moved down to San Francisco in 1937, took hold of the company there, separated it from the opera, and became its *maître*. If Lew was the finest dancer of the three brothers, Harold was the master teacher and Willam the entrepreneur, the impresario, the leader. All three were courageous and confident, but those early years in San Francisco saw Willam fearless in the face of imminent disaster more than once.

In 1939, Willam decided that the large, ballet-mad Russian community of San Francisco deserved a whole evening of dance. Until he took over, the ballet company had been a part of the opera, just as in Europe for centuries, and Willam was determined that it was now time to present "the real thing," a full-length ballet. *Coppelia* was his choice. "I had to learn *Coppelia* the hard way," he says with a chuckle. "We got the music for acts one and two, but we couldn't get act three." Willam had received permission to stage the ballet, though, and he was not going to be thwarted. "We had the conductor orchestrate the rest in the style of Delibes [the composer]," he says, and *Coppelia*'s concluding act was reborn.

Two years later Willam and his devoted little troupe of dancers were in danger; they had come back from touring four thousand dollars in the hole. Something had to be done, and fast. Informal opinion gathering—by Willam and his friends—had proved that ballet-goers in San Francisco were salivating for a full-length *Swan Lake*. Christiansen was told no, no, no, no, and no by his bosses, but he was determined to give them

Swan Lake. "Now, this was guts," he says forty-four years later, warming to the tale with sparkling eyes. "I told President Merola that I would take full artistic *and* financial responsibility. Then I rented a loft where we painted the scenery. We did everything, and Lew came out to play Siegfried." The house sold out, and *Swan Lake* was a smash. "I had to do something," says Willam. "My job was to do ballets and help dancers, and I had dancers on my hands who had to eat."

In 1944, San Francisco balletomanes saw the first-ever American *Nutcracker*. Before staging the loved work, Willam spent hours with Balanchine and Danilova, eliciting memories of the St. Petersburg *Nutcracker* of their youth. That was the *Nutcracker* Willam wanted for America and for all the Russians in San Francisco: the original version. His reincarnation wowed all who saw it; it also marked the beginning of America's possessiveness toward the ballet. Though his old company has a newer version of the work now, Willam's *Nuts* is still being danced elsewhere, and it is still a guaranteed hit.

In his earliest years in San Francisco, Willam still danced; later he used his brothers and their ballerina wives as regularly as possible. When war economies threatened the school with closure, Willam and Harold bought the place. Harold had already established himself as a respected teacher, so he was put in charge; he ran the SFBS until he retired in 1975. Like Willam, Harold had married his partner from the vaudeville days. Lew's bride was a dancer he had met at SAB, Gisella Caccialanza.

Gisella was from California, but as a young girl she had been sent to Italy to study with Enrico Cecchetti. Her relationship with the Italian master grew so close that he was even named her godfather. From Milan, Gisella journeyed to

New York to study with Balanchine, who, of course, had also studied with Cecchetti—but not in Italy and not in Russia, where Nijinsky had met the maestro and ballet Italian-style. Balanchine came under Cecchetti's tutelage in France, after Diaghilev brought the Italian over to coach his Ballets Russes dancers. "I'm my own Grandpa," indeed. The world of classical dance is very, very small.

Lew and Gisella were a couple to be envied—a golden twosome. They were beautiful, strong, and talented; they were entangled with the exciting Russian and the birth of American ballet; and they were very much in love. In 1951, they went west. Willam was moving to Utah, so Lew took over as San Francisco's director, a post he held until his death in 1985. Lew brought with him to the Coast a first-class dancer and teacher in Gisella, and he also brought along his strong and happy ties to Balanchine and Kirstein. Soon an alliance between the companies and schools formed. San Francisco dancers did Balanchine's choreography, and the New York City Ballet staged *Filling Station*. Stars of each company made guest appearances with the other, and the main beneficiaries of the cooperation were the public, who saw more ballet, broader ballet, better ballet. The Christiansens, Balanchine, and Kirstein proved that East and West could not only meet, they could share, and all would be stronger for it.

City Ballet dancer Larry Matthews grew up in California, graduated from the San Francisco Ballet School, and rose to the level of principal with Willam and Lew's company before heading east. Says he of Lew Christiansen, "Lew was a drill sergeant. When you thought your guts were falling out, he would ask you to do more. Once I left to go study in Holland. I stayed exactly twelve days before coming back to

Lew. I didn't realize just how much he had to offer until I went away."

In 1952, Willam Christiansen started a ballet department at the University of Utah, out of which would be born Ballet West, an exuberant and vital professional ballet company. Both the school and Ballet West still shine like beacons through nearby states, drawing male dancers from the most unlikely sources. Michael Smuin came from Montana so that he could become Gene Kelly; Tom Ruud arrived from Wyoming; and Salt Lake City sent its own homegrown sons, Bart Cook and Tracy Bennett, to Willam. The boys all learned ballet Christiansen-style. Willam taught a strict, tough class, pounding out the counts on the floor with a stick and demanding the same energy and strength that his brothers were insisting upon in San Francisco. Willam also made sure that his boys danced like boys. Says he with characteristic modesty, "I'm expert at training the male dancer."

Recalls Tracy Bennett, "I'm not even sure how he did it. All those tricks. He just said do them, and we did them: double tours, sauts de basque. You name it. He would also stop class regularly and tell us stories about when he was studying Cecchetti technique. He talked with reverence about it." High leaps and fast spins are vital to the Christiansen/West Coast style of dancing. All those tricks. The emphasis is heavy on virtuosity, more so than on the perfect fifth position, extreme turnouts, and exact placement that marks the Stanley Williams/East Coast–trained dancer, on mass of muscle rather than long sinews. Says Bennett, "Willam used to yell at us if we stretched. He told us we would lose our jumps." Says Willam, "Men have to look like men onstage. I don't give a darn what they are as long as they look manly on stage."

In 1976, Michael Smuin was made codirector, with Lew, of the San Francisco Ballet. Smuin had danced in nightclubs and on Broadway, and with American Ballet Theatre. He was mostly a *demicharactère* dancer (the second banana; the straight man who doesn't always get the girl but who does get wonderful steps), and he performed with skill and humor, particularly in ballets like *Fancy Free*, Jerome Robbins's American classic that features three sailors out on the town. Smuin has always been very theatrical, and during his nine years of directing and choreographing in San Francisco, he made a number of glossy, show-bizzy, very popular works and did some dances for television and the movies. Now, though, says Willam Christiansen, "America is turning back to classicism." Ballet West reached into Danish dance history in 1985 and revived a Bournonville ballet, *Abdallah*, and the same year San Francisco changed directors, from the glitzy Smuin to Helgi Tomasson, a Danish-trained former NYCB dancer and a choreographer of Mozartean purity.

When Michael Smuin left New York to join Lew in 1973, he brought more with him from the East than just his bulging bag of balletic tricks. During New York auditions Smuin had hired a promising teenager for the company's corps. The kid was studying with Michael's next-door neighbor, Richard Thomas. He was only sixteen; he was just 5'7" and a bit stocky, but it was thought he would be good at the kinds of parts Michael had always excelled in. Lew didn't agree; he thought the boy was just too young, but Michael prevailed, and Sean Lavery left for San Francisco.

Lavery is now 6'1½", devoid of baby fat, and a premier danseur with the New York City Ballet. His Roman profile is accompanied by a wide American smile and topped with a head full of blond curls. Lavery is as elegant a *danseur noble* as

America has ever produced; he has an easy classicism and is blessed with a huge jump, a whirlwind turn, and a knowing hand. He is a partner of unusual strength and sensitivity. He is also a nice Irish boy from football-mad Harrisburg, Pennsylvania.

Lavery started ballet lessons when he was ten, and he carefully concealed the fact from his schoolmates for as long as he could. "Are you kidding?" he says. "They made fun of the *girls* who took dance lessons!" Although he was swimming competitively, Lavery did not come to ballet through his sport. Nor did he come because his mother dragged him, or because his sister danced. He came because he wanted to, because he had to. When Sean was ten, his family took him to see a neighbor's daughter in a performance of *Sleeping Beauty*. He was thunderstruck. "I went nuts," he recalls. "I thought, 'This is something I must do.' " His mother remembers that she lost track of her son for a little while after they had all gone backstage to congratulate their neighbor on her performance. When Mrs. Lavery went looking for Sean, she found him in the middle of the stage, gazing dreamily around as though in a trance.

Lisa de Ribere, an admired dancer with ABT and now a choreographer, was the girl next door. She took lessons with Marcia Dale Weary in nearby Carlisle, the town with the Indian reservation where Jim Thorpe gained his football-playing fame. In that unlikely locale lies a school of high standards, with a committed and obsessed director. Sean rushed over to Ms. Weary's Harrisburg school and enrolled immediately. "I was the only boy in the class," he says, "but I didn't care. I took six or seven classes a week. I was as serious as can be; I was just so anxious to learn to jump and turn and to stick a girl up on my shoulder!"

After a few months with Ms. Weary, Lavery added the Pennsylvania Ballet School to his roster of responsibilities, traveling the more than two hundred miles to and from Philadelphia weekly for additional instruction. The first summer after he started lessons he spent two solid weeks in the City of Brotherly Love and took classes with lots of other boys. It is always a shock for a talented boy who is used to being the only one to come upon a roomful of others like himself. Some are pleased; some, like Max, get intimidated. All get their competitive juices flowing. Lavery was a kid with a mission, and he was not going to be outdone by anyone else. One day he would learn a complicated combination ending with a pirouette, and the next day he would double the number of turns, always fueling his own fires with an inner voice that nagged, "You'll never be a dancer; you're ugly and you're terrible." Within a year he was questioning his teacher as to why on earth he was being taught the corps part of *Swan Lake;* he only intended to dance Siegfried, the male lead. He was eleven at the time. His teacher assured him she was only having him learn the lesser role "in case you want to teach when you retire."

By the time he was in the seventh grade, Lavery had discovered how much he loved ballet, and he had also found out how much the road he had chosen would cost him. His schedule was grueling and exhausting, and he had given up swimming and all other after-school activities. Then his secret got out; everyone knew he was taking ballet lessons, and he lost most of his pals. "Even the girls were cruel," he says. "I didn't have many friends, and there were lots of fights and bloody noses. I was called a lot of names. I tried to say to myself, 'Who needs 'em? They're ignorant.' But it got lonely; I felt very alone."

The time was the late sixties, in Harrisburg, Pennsylvania . . . before the ballet boom thundered across America. It would be easier for Lavery today. More kids would have seen ballet, would envy his opportunities, would be proud to be associated with him. It will never be the same as quarterbacking the high-school football team; dance will never interest as many people as football does. And adolescents who are different from the pack will always seem odd to some of their peers. It matters a lot less now, though. American boys have numbers on their side in the eighties, and they have a dance history of their own, complete with representatives in the uniquely American aristocracy of television and movie stars. When Sean Lavery was a kid, though, even the adults were nasty about his being a dancer. His worst experience came at the hand of a teacher, a fine setter of examples for the students. It was in seventh-grade geography. The news of Sean's outside activity had just buzzed around the school. The teacher announced to the class that young Lavery was studying ballet, then made the boy stand in front of the room while he led everyone else in an enforced chorus of "Tiptoe Through the Tulips." The memory still brings a hard edge to Lavery's usually velvety voice.

When he turned thirteen, Lavery left Harrisburg behind and emigrated to New York, to study with Richard Thomas (John Boy's father) and to live with Thomas and his wife, the late Barbara Fallis. It was hard for Mrs. Lavery to let her son move. She wanted him to have every chance to pursue the dancing that he loved so much, but she was frightened. She didn't know what to expect, and in her experience boys that young left home for only one reason, to join a religious order. "When I drove Sean over to the Thomases," she says, "I felt that I was delivering him into the priesthood. It was as though I was losing him forever. I cried all the way home to Harrisburg."

Sean Lavery's mother did not lose her son, but she wasn't far wrong in comparing his life to that of a seminarian. Lincoln Kirstein's comparison is more specific; he says dancers live like Jesuits. It's an accurate analogy. Members of the Society of Jesus are the most worldly men of the cloth. They are the elite. Beautifully educated and cultured, they partake richly of many of life's pleasures; fine food and wine, travel, theater, and music are all available to Jesuits. Yet they are priests. There is a serious dedication to a higher principle, and there are sacrifices. Their lives are choreographed by others, and they always have a core of singularity, of aloneness. They live for something besides themselves. Dancers' lives are single-minded, single-purposed, devoted to a higher principle. Perfection is defined for dancers as for priests; their ideal is clear, and it is something they must daily aspire to, always with an understanding of their own particular strengths and weaknesses.

Dancers are as obedient as priests too; they are at the mercy of choreographers and ballet masters who make decisions for them. They cannot take control; they must accept others' dictates. There is no democracy in ballet. Every day starts with class for everyone, no matter what level of luminary. Then there are rehearsals, costume fittings, physical therapists, chiropractors, work on ballets in progress, special strength-building workouts, photo sessions. Then performances and guest appearances. A dancer's workday normally begins at ten A.M. and ends around eleven P.M., when the one real meal can be consumed. During performing seasons dancers have one day off a week, one day to fit in managers, accountants, analysts, friends, shopping, cleaning, sleeping late, going to the movies, taking a walk, writing letters, paying bills, and having personal relationships.

Students of dance are like novices, eager to become full-fledged monks. They, too, pledge obedience; they, too, give control completely over to someone else. With students it's to the teacher. Blind faith and trust are required. Sometimes the relationship takes place fully in the classroom; other times it is more personal, more intense, more concentrated, more like athlete and coach. Coaches can put their jocks on tracks that will lead to fine schools and lucrative professional careers, or to medals of gold at Olympic competitions. Teachers can give dancers the key to the star's dressing room, can head them toward careers filled with applause and adulation. Both can also cause serious harm. Absolute power can corrupt absolutely; there are always abuses of the teacher/student or coach/athlete balance. Dancers and players can be pushed too hard; too much can be asked of them, and serious physical damage can be inflicted on them. Psychological stress can also take a heavy toll on young emotions, and there are tales of sexual abuse perpetrated on both girls and boys.

Most of the time in ballet, student and teacher have the same goal; most of the time the relationship is supportive, not destructive. There are meanies and nuts and chicken hawks out there, though. Parents shouldn't panic about the fact, however, because there are probably far fewer abuses of students at ballet schools than at boarding schools or in the kids' own homes.

Ballet students start young and can burn out young, especially the boys. Somewhere in mid-adolescence they get bored with it; they chafe at being so obedient and so disciplined, so sacrificing and directed, so not in control of their own lives. They get tired of hurting and failing. That's when the kids wonder why on earth they are going through all this, why they are working so hard, and why they have been doing so for so long. Says Mrs. Gleboff, "Certainly they begin to wonder if this is what they want, especially if they started very young. Yet they feel they've put in so many years, and they don't know where to turn. It takes courage." Like Max, Sean Lavery was fifteen when he had his rebellious fling. His was not violent, though; he only hurt himself.

By the time he arrived in New York, Sean had been working hard every day of every week for three years. He had a large talent, a voracious desire, recognizable ability, and a knee that was starting to go. It was great to be the special one at the Thomases' school, the chosen one, the one who lived with the teacher. It was also terrific to be at PCS. What a difference from Harrisburg. All his schoolmates either acted or sang or danced; they were all actually impressed with him too. What a joy. What a relief. Soon his friends became very important to him, more important than anything else. Again Mrs. Gleboff: "The boys have more of a tendency to want to be popular at all costs, even negative costs." Sean's friends were wilder than any of the kids he had known at home, more daring, much more sophisticated. They were exciting. Soon he started skipping class with his pals, hanging out at Fordham University, across the street from PCS, smoking cigarettes and drinking Cokes. The Cherub as Adolescent. Other kids take drugs or drink vodka, flunk academics, and stay out late at discos. Some quit dancing altogether.

No matter how one acts out, though, what form of recklessness or abuse the teenage dancer decides to inflict on his body and psyche, it can't last for long without the piper demanding his pay. Dancers can't hide; abuses show—fast. Soon Sean's rebellion was obvious to one and all. His dancing started to suffer; he was becoming less special, less able. That he couldn't stand. Nothing was worth that. "I just grew up and wanted better," he says. He finished PCS by correspondence although he lived just a few short blocks away, worked hard at the barre, and at sixteen left for San Francisco, a job, and a salary. It was his chance, he felt, and he was right.

XI.

Role Models

Max was sixteen when he went to San Francisco, too, and like Sean, he viewed his time out West as a chance at a new balletic existence. Max wouldn't have a job or a salary, but he would be away from New York, away from home, away from his teachers, Mrs. Gleboff, and his reputation. Or so he thought. What he didn't realize was that when you go away from home, you don't just pack your new leotards and slippers. Your smelly old sweats sneak into your bag, too, unfolded and unpressed. All the junk one wants to leave behind, all the troubles, joys, fears, and angers just come right along too. Sometimes a change of air can dilute the old stuff, can freshen it, but a mere airplane ride can't get rid of it.

When Sean Lavery was first in San Francisco, he turned into a self-described "party monster" who regularly stayed up much later than he ever had and who greeted the dawn through a haze of assorted controlled substances. It was his first time on his own, and he behaved like a new fraternity member. He says he wouldn't trade those days of early independence for anything and that his West Coast friends are his closest to this day. During Max's first weeks in San

Francisco he displayed what his teachers called "attitude problems." He acted as though he were better than anyone else, as though he knew more than the instructors. He paid little attention to corrections, and less to the dress code. All his classes were mixed, boys and girls, and all the girls were younger than he. He showed off to them and loved pushing ahead to the front of the room, a truly obnoxious breach of ballet etiquette. When in doubt, act out. Max was scared; he wanted to make good, he really did, but he was afraid of showing it. He was also afraid of showing the fact that he was homesick, that he wanted his Mommy. Maybe if the other boys from SAB hadn't been there, he would have been less self-conscious, but his first days in San Francisco were like his first days at SAB.

After a couple of weeks, though, Max was finding his new chance. One of his teachers, Helen Koop, made him feel safe in class and more available to instruction. Says Max, "San Francisco taught me discipline." Soon he missed home less, although every time he did something well, he wished his mother were there to see it. It was fun living in the dorm, and he even made some new friends. Every Friday night there would be a beach party. They had an eleven P.M. curfew, but until then they sat around bonfires, drank beer, and generally felt very on their own. Max got to practice making out with a couple of girls over the six weeks, and he was even able to curve his hand around a burgeoning breast and stroke a sinewy thigh once or twice. All in all, it turned out to be a real good summer.

Max didn't like traveling around San Francisco, though. "On Saturday nights you couldn't even go out," he says with a sour expression of disgust. His blond good looks and sensuous face were too much for some members of the city's large homosexual community, and he had to rebuff more than one attempted pickup. "Faggots," he says, shuddering.

Max and his friends can't stand homosexuals. Most adolescent boys find sexuality—homo or hetero—confusing, appealing, and scary. These boys are no different, but their reaction to homosexuals is more intense. They are with more gay men than others their age, and they have all been called names by some clod. These are boys on the cusp, still unsure about their own sexuality. They have not yet firmly rooted themselves in heterosexual relationships, and they often think people are going to assume they are gay. So, overcompensation sets in. "Not me, no, certainly not me," they are saying. "See? To prove it I will show you how much I despise those damn faggots." To one extroverted, friendly homosexual in his class, an ebullient chatterer and patter of arms, Max once angrily shouted, "Keep your hands off me!" The classmate was surprised and a little startled, but not really hurt. He knew the words said more about their speaker and his insecurities than about him and his intentions.

It's not that all homosexual dancers do or do not come on to boys in the dressing room or classroom. Some do and some don't. Sometimes a homosexual teacher or older professional dancer will use his position of power to gain the favors of a boy who interests him. Sometimes a gay youth will pursue a classmate of his own age, but rarely without some mutuality.

There are, of course, many homosexual dancers. There are also homosexual doctors, lawyers, and professional football players, and there are now plenty of heterosexual dancers, too—more than ever before because of a broader acceptance of ballet. You don't have to be gay to dance, and homosexuality is not contagious. Max was not going to "catch" it from anyone he knew, or be lured into a depraved life-style, either. No one had ever groped Max in the locker room or tried to entice him in any way—except for one or two of the girls. No teacher had ever hinted at the slightest sexual interest in him, and no older dancer had ever suggested as much as a shared cup of coffee. Max had nothing to fear but fear itself.

Brenda Fuqua has made very clear her feelings about homosexuals to her son. She takes a born-again biblical stance. She believes homosexuality is sinful, and she doesn't want her son being friendly with any gays because, she says, he would thereby indicate approval of their way of life, and he should always show disapproval. The irony is, though, that Max doesn't really know who is gay and who isn't.

Usually, after they have grown up, gay and straight dancers have a gentle tolerance for each other that could serve as a model for the world outside. Coexistence and understanding are the cornerstones, acceptance and tolerance the cement. Strong friendships go unthreatened by opposite sexual preferences, and sometimes gay and straight men even share apartments—respectfully, successfully, and happily. Max and some of his friends are still sure that gays are "gross," however, and that they have to show the world regularly that they are not of or with them.

Before he spent the summer in San Francisco, Max had been dying to get his own apartment. His friends Andrew and Rob shared a place on West Seventy-fourth in New York. Brian lived with them, too, but Brian is no longer a student. He is now with the City Ballet, and he pretty much goes his own way. Drew and Rob are the real roomies. They have a ball; they do exactly as they please. They stay out late; they drink beer and smoke what and when they feel like smoking; and neither has a mother constantly keeping tabs on him as Max does, appearing at school and embarrassing him. If he lived with Rob and Drew, Max could do whatever he wanted. He would really be free, answering to no one. It sounded like heaven.

By the time he got home from California, he'd changed his mind. He didn't want all that independence. He needed home. He needed his mother. In San Francisco he'd enjoyed the dorm life, but he'd had enough. Out there he'd played every trick that every new camper or college freshman plays. He was the king of the short sheet; the duke of furniture piling; the earl of staying up late and making noise. The decibel level in the SAB boys' part of the dorm was roughly that which accompanies an SST's smash through the sound barrier. Max had fallen back in love with dance out in San Francisco, too, and he'd felt successful for the first time in a long time. He loved character dancing. He thought the polkas and czardas were fun and that heel clicking and shouting "Hah" was a trip. He also really got into his regular ballet sessions, particularly with Ms. Koop. She made him feel so much better about himself, and he really wanted to show her how good he could be. Max responded better to women. He worked hard for her and he worked well, and at the end of the session it was the opinion of all his West Coast teachers that in spite of his early adjustment problems, he was a student with real potential.

When Sean Lavery lived in San Francisco, he shared half a house with three other dancers. The oldest was eighteen. As the roommates scoured the city to find a place to live, they were regularly turned down by landlords claiming they were sorry but they didn't allow pets or children. Sean earned seventy-five dollars a week and thought he was pretty

damned adult. In fact, he was, in spite of his party-mon-
stering. While others his age were at college, worrying about
grades and dances and sports, he was pursuing his career and
amassing practical skills. He learned to cook, how to get
around a new city, to shop, to manage money, and generally
how to take care of himself. "I loved being on my own," he
recalls. He didn't love being used onstage infrequently,
however, and then just for character parts, such as the old
jeweler in Lew Christiansen's *Cinderella,* complete with huge
bags painted under his teenage eyes and a black beard pasted
on his downy chin. He wanted to dance. This was, after all,
the same Sean Lavery who had been unable to understand, at
the age of eleven, why he was supposed to learn a corps role.
Within a year he returned to New York, taller, thinner, not
much older, but a lot wiser.

He intended to seek his fortune at American Ballet
Theatre but instead went to Germany, to dance in Frankfurt.
Four of his friends were there, and the fivesome struggled
along together. They danced like crazy, and they never had
anywhere near enough money; they even had to rely on
gathering deposit bottles to pay for food to eat. Christmas saw
the knot of depressed Yanks huddled together, listening to
Armed Forces radio. They had no roast goose, no tall Tannen-
baum, not even a TV to numb their blues. Still, Lavery says,
"It was the most influential and important time in my life. I
grew up in Germany. I made good friends there, and I found a
way to laugh at everything. And, boy, did I learn. I was in
nineteen of twenty-one ballets, and we also did operas. The
first year I was a soloist, and the second a principal. They
threw me into *Sleeping Beauty* with eight days to learn the
lead. 'Figure it out and get out there and do it,' they said. I
thought it was great. I loved every minute of it."

Or almost every minute of it. It was in Frankfurt that

Sean Lavery in *Sleeping Beauty* (Frankfurt).

Sean danced with his first terrorizing ballerina, and the experience almost stopped him from staying on for a second year. Though common usage permits the term *ballerina* to apply to any female classical dancer, only stars, principals, fit the true definition of the word; the rest are just dancers. Lavery had been in partnering classes since he was young and yearning to "stick a girl up on my shoulder." He had had some wonderful times with his partners in San Francisco, and he had learned a great deal about how to do it, how to adjust to each different dancer's balance, how to help each do steps she could not do without him, how to present her to the audience as fully and attractively as possible. He had always felt that he and his partner were a team, an entry, and all the girls he had danced with felt the same way.

In Germany he met one for storybooks. She was a Brunhild with an acid tongue and a disposition to match. She yelled at him for mistakes he made and for some she made herself. She humiliated him in front of the rest of the company, and she corrected his slightest variance with a barrage of insults. Only his anger kept him going. He'd show her, he vowed. He was not going to let her spoil everything for him. Talking about her now, he chuckles. "She certainly wasn't like Patty McBride. Patty is one of the greatest ballerinas ever, and one of the sweetest. 'Oh, Sean,' she'll say in her little-girl voice, 'would you mind just moving your hands down here just a little bit? Oh, thank you.' I had no idea there were stars like her. I thought at first that they would all be like that awful woman in Germany."

After his European tour of duty, Lavery returned to the States and signed up with Columbia Artists. Shades of the Christiansen brothers. Lavery's troup didn't stop at vaudeville houses, though; they never played the Palace, and they didn't share their bill with anyone, much less Jack Benny. This was a full ballet tour via bus, for eight weeks at a time. Every day it was into a new city, take a class, then put on a performance. Itinerant troubadors had nothing on this group. "Every night we did the *Corsair* pas de deux, and then we did three other ballets," says Lavery. "Then we'd wash out our tights ourselves and go to bed. In the morning we'd get back on the bus and go on to the next city. We'd get to the next place, take a class, then put on a performance. Night after night after night. We never even got to look at the scenery, because we were so tired we always slept on the bus. It would be, 'Oh, there's the Grand Canyon. Look. Huh? What? Oh, yeah.' Glimpse out the window. Then back to sleep. Sometimes there would be receptions. That would be our dinner: grape jelly meatball hors d'oeuvres and Jell-O. Mostly we danced in high-school auditoriums. We never had a linoleum stage. It was killing on our feet and legs and on our backs. We played Cody, Wyoming; Gallup, New Mexico; and Scott's Bluff, Nebraska. We brought ballet to towns that had never even considered classical dance. I know it's corny to say, but doing that tour, you really felt you were doing something for ballet."

In between eight-week jaunts Lavery auditioned for the NYCB. He had learned a number of Balanchine ballets in Germany, and he wanted to dance for Mr. B. To get into a ballet company, though, you don't send your résumé or call up and say, "Gee, Mr. Balanchine, I'd like a job." You take a class. Maybe several classes. That's how you audition. Sean sauntered over to SAB and took what he thought was Stanley Williams's class, only Krammie was the teacher. The next day he took company class, the daily ninety-minute session for the pros. Balanchine came into the studio, saw the tall blond man with two shoes, and an invitation was extended.

The company was about to embark on a between-seasons tour; they asked Lavery if he could come to Washington with them. Though he was dying to join the group, though he had just been offered what he viewed as his latest chance of a lifetime, the loyal Lavery said no. He had promised that he would do another small-town America tour for another eight weeks, and so he boarded the bus and joined the NYCB on his return. Though he'd been a principal dancer in Germany and the number-one star on his Feet Across America tour, at City Ballet Lavery started in the corps and was happy to do so.

He proceeded to establish a new speed record for promotion, though, rushing from corps to soloist in a year and rocketing to principal rank a mere four months later. Now he is a premier danseur; he dances all the starring parts once inhabited by Lew Christiansen, Jacques d'Amboise, and Peter Martins, and also has several works that were choreographed especially for him.

In November 1985, Lavery danced his first *Apollo* at Lincoln Center's New York State Theater. He had done the coveted work in Europe, in Minneapolis, and even upstate in Saratoga, the NYCB's summer home, but he had never been permitted to dance it in Manhattan. And he had been dying to. One cold Friday night he had his chance. He was excited beyond belief and almost paralyzed with terror. He knew he would forget every step; he was sure he would fall or drop his partner, or both, and otherwise totally disgrace himself.

Just before he went on, Lincoln Kirstein said to him, "Remember, you're a dinosaur," meaning that he was now a part of ballet history, but Lavery couldn't decide whether he was being told he was big and clumsy or that he had a tiny brain or that he would soon be extinct. Then he heard the first notes of the music and forgot his worries. He forgot who he was and where he was, and he became a young god, cavorting on Olympus with his muses. His efforts drew repeated curtain calls and cries of bravo, also his first rave reviews from *New York Times* critic Anna Kisselgoff, who had until then been lukewarm toward the Pennsylvanian deity. The next morning saw Lavery at SAB, quietly taking class among the students. Krammie was teaching. He asked Sean what they had per-

Sean Lavery as
Apollo in New
York.

formed the night before. When he heard "*Apollo*," he queried
who had danced the lead. Lavery said, "I did," and Krammie
stood at attention, raised his eyebrows, and bowed in tribute.
It took twenty seconds, then class continued. Even *Apollo* is
not exempt from the danseur's ritual.

Another dancer who came to New York from San
Francisco is Larry Matthews. Matthews is like an elegant elf.
His large eyes give him a look of constant delighted surprise.

Matthews is a sunny dancer, a gentle gentleman. He was a principal in San Francisco who joined NYCB in the corps. Larry and his wife, Tina (who became a dancer only after having been a nun), left the West Coast just as Michael Smuin and Sean Lavery were arriving. They were newlyweds then, and together they set out to conquer the East. Their first stop was Philadelphia and the Pennsylvania Ballet.

Barbara Weissberger, the founder of the Pennsylvania Ballet (and the more recent Carlisle Choreography Project), was the first child to come under George Balanchine's tutelage at SAB, and it was under the maestro's aegis that she started the Philadelphia company. Balanchine sent her dancers and ballets; his choreography became the heart of her repertoire.

Philadelphia had always been hospitable to classical dance. George Washington Smith was from Philadelphia. The Littlefield sisters started the first all-American company there, and visiting luminaries had stopped there first for many years. It was appropriate for the City of Brotherly Love to become the first Balanchinian outpost beyond New York. How appropriate also that another Balanchine dancer, Robert Weiss, is now in charge of the company and that Peter Martins is his adviser.

In 1973, it was Mrs. Weissberger who hired both Larry and Tina to dance with the company. Larry looks back and laughs now. "We were so naive, and we had trouble getting used to such a different way of living. We are both Californians; during our first winter storm we called Barbara and said we couldn't come to work because our car was covered in snow. She said, *'Whaaaat?'*"

Larry and Tina weren't happy in Philadelphia, and they soon moved to New York, with hopes high that spots would be available for both of them at City Ballet. Alas,

Balanchine had room only for Larry, and that in the corps. At first Tina just stayed in their apartment, sobbed, and watched reruns of *The Streets of San Francisco* on television. Eventually she pulled herself together, accepted her fate, and became a teacher; she now specializes in bringing back dancers from injury.

Back in Larry's early City Ballet days, he would come home and describe what had gone on in class, what Mr. Balanchine had taught them and what he had asked of them. Stunned, Tina would stammer, "But—but . . . that's humanly impossible."

"It was hard at first, playing catch-up," says Larry. "It had been a nice isolation being on the West Coast. It enabled me to have a complete lack of doubt. I'd never played sports, and I wasn't really very strong, but I hadn't realized it. If I'd known when I was a principal out West that Peter Martins and the others were dancing the same *Nutcracker* pas de deux that I was . . ."

Larry Matthews is still in the City Ballet corps, and he has no desire to do anything else. "It's hard to top this for an interesting job," he says. "It's so much fun in so many ways. David Richardson, who danced in the corps for years and years, told me that this can be the best time, that this is what I've worked for. He was right. Had I not been a principal in San Francisco, I might have felt more determined to get promoted here. But I've done principal parts, and besides, I wasn't the nicest person I knew in San Francisco.

"Being involved with dancing is a way of life," Matthews continues, "a very special way of life. You're allowed to keep alive some of your youthfulness when you're a dancer. I seem to be alive in a kind of way that I wasn't brought up to expect from adulthood."

XII.

Friends

When Max returned to New York from San Francisco, he was filled with resolve. He was going to make good at SAB, and he was definitely going to stay out of trouble there. His visit with his father on his way back had helped motivate him. As usual, Pappy wanted Max to forget this ballet stuff, to get serious, to come back to "real life" and Dallas and Highland Park High. He also wanted his son to come work in his health-food store. Max would sooner do a thousand tendus, a million pliés; he'd even rather obey SAB's dress code. He was not going to go back to Texas, no matter what.

After leaving Dallas, Max stopped off in Albuquerque to say hello to his brothers and sisters. Lana, the eldest, had moved there when she married a Western-style painter. Louis followed after a time. After he graduated from high school Louis had headed for Hawaii, where he spent his days bodybuilding and his nights pulling tourists around Waikiki in the island's version of a rickshaw. Then he moved to Switzerland, where he lived and studied with a theologian of his father's acquaintance. That's where Louis found himself and found his answers. That's where he got intensely involved in his religion. Alice joined the others in Albuquerque after giving New York a try. She had moved East with Max and company, but she couldn't live with all of them and couldn't afford a place of her own. Nothing came together for Alice. She had finished high school in Dallas, but she was not going to college. She had to earn some money, but she had no training. And she got herself involved in a heartbreaking love affair with an older man. Religion didn't help her, and she wouldn't stay in therapy. Alice was a real worry to her mother, and a real pain in the neck to Max, who viewed her as a professional victim. She was the youngest of the Mullen offspring and by far the most unhappy of Brenda Fuqua's children. Brenda was glad when Alice decided to go to New Mexico; she thought she'd be better off there.

Stephen was in Albuquerque too. Etienne. He's the eldest Fuqua. Stephen tried living with his father and with his mother. Then he moved in with Louis. He liked Albuquerque High, even though he was a couple of years behind others his age. Says his mother, "Etienne doesn't test well, but he is not stupid. He's very cunning."

Max had always done as well in school as he wanted to. He was bright enough, a good reader, able to think, and able to question. He could be a lively and informed student or a lazy, neglectful one. It all depended on his mood. If he didn't want to do something, he didn't do it. Nothing could make him do it. "You know me," he says with a shrug. Mostly he thought it was all a crock, but he wasn't a true troublemaker. Only twice had he gotten into messes; once was with Josh at SAB and the other back in Dallas, when he argued "to the death" with his seventh-grade science teacher about evolution. Max took the creationist opposition stance. He wouldn't give up; he carried on and carried on. Finally he was sent to the principal, who then sent him home—for two weeks. He was just as unrepentant then as he was about Josh. Each time he felt fully justified in his action.

Correspondence school was a total loss for Max. He carried the books and notes around and looked the part of a real student, but that was all. So far he'd accumulated, after a whole academic year, no credits. He'd lost a full year.

The new start Max felt he had made in California got a bit shaky when he came home to find nothing changed. He had to face everything he had left behind: the same schoolwork, the same Intermediate class, the same corrections. He wasn't sure he could continue to do it. Thank heaven he had his job running for Charlie.

In her book about SAB, *New York Times* critic Jennifer Dunning calls Charlie "an unofficial mascot." Walking into the school, it would be easy to assume that he's in charge, that he runs things. Charlie answers the telephones. Charlie welcomes the pros who come in to take class, always by name and always commenting on their performances of the night before. Charlie chats with the mothers, scolds young dancers who, he thinks, need to drop a few pounds or try a bit harder, and rubs the necks of those in pain. Every year Charlie gives himself a birthday present by taking a small group of his favorite aspiring ballerinas out for dinner and champagne. "I take only the ones who listen to me," he says, "and I always buy good champagne. The good stuff won't give them headaches." Says one of Charlie's girls, former SAB'er, now NYC-B'er Sharon Hershfield, "He's my grandfather."

Charlie is in his mid-sixties. He's of medium height and slim, he has thinning dark hair and very dark eyes (one of which doesn't work right), and he almost always has a cigarette dangling from the side of his mouth. Charlie grew up in an Orthodox Jewish home in Brooklyn, but you would never guess so. Charlie also had a wife and two children, but you probably wouldn't guess that, either: he seems such a loner. Charlie was also, at one time in his life, a major-league gambler. That you might guess.

Charlie came to ballet through the kitchen door, not the back door. Events in his life had conspired to rid him of his wife and kids and his career, and Charlie found himself living in the Empire Hotel and working in the hotel's coffee shop. The Empire is across the street from the New York State Theater, where the City Ballet plies its magic, and three blocks down Broadway from the Juilliard building, where SAB trains the magicians. All the dancers dropped into the coffee shop at one time or another. George Balanchine used to frequent the place too. Charlie has never been known for his shy, retiring manner, so soon he knew all the dancers and was engaging Mr. B. in conversation regularly too. He and the master would talk about music, about food, about vodka, and about ballet. Says Charlie, "Mr. Balanchine would answer questions from anyone, no matter who and no matter how stupid. Once I told him I had really enjoyed a ballet of his the night before, the one called *Dances at a Gathering*. Mr. Balanchine just quietly said, 'That's a Jerome Robbins ballet.' I thought I would die."

Charlie knows all the ushers at the State Theater and at the other Lincoln Center theaters too. Almost every night of the year Charlie sees great dance or hears fabulous music, all of it, as he would say, *à la maison*. Sometimes one can even find him first at the State Theater viewing a favorite dancer in a new role, then at the Met, checking out the latest ABT discovery, and finally at Avery Fisher Hall for a finale of some blockbuster Beethoven. After such a filled evening, all Charlie has to do is cross the street to the Empire and he's home, and during the day he's surrounded by all the beautiful and talented youngsters at SAB. There are worse ways to live, that's for sure. Says Charlie, "The arts were the best thing that ever happened to me. With the arts there's a beginning and no end."

Charlie takes his favorite girls to more than a yearly champagne-filled dinner. Often they see their first concert and opera with him, and the most favored of the favorites get a trip to the racetrack. It's not unusual for horse lovers to be balletomanes and vice versa; it must have something to do with all those legs.

After years of volunteer service Charlie was put on SAB's payroll. He's the school's traffic director. What that means is that Charlie is the major gofer. If it needs picking up or delivering, if it needs to be rushed to the theater for a signature and then zoomed back to the school in a trice, Charlie is the man to summon. Charlie is in charge of the SAB messengers, all of whom are students who work shifts that won't interfere with their ballet classes.

Max got his job with Charlie just a few days before he did his job on Josh. Sidney Charles Wigler would never admit it, but one senses he was trying to help a boy headed for trouble when he hired Max. Max hadn't been doing anything for months, and he also never had enough money for slippers or tights or anything else. He was also running very low on self-esteem. Charlie hired him, and Charlie maintains to one and all, "Max? He's the greatest. You can trust Max with your life."

In the fall, after he came back from San Francisco, Max went back to work for Charlie. And back to class at SAB. Five days a week, Monday through Friday, from ten A.M. to two P.M., Max worked as one of Charlie's boys. On duty he roamed the city, by taxi, bus, subway, and foot. He delivered invitations to the school's annual fund-raising party at fancy Park Avenue apartments and butlered brownstones. He got glimpses of swank penthouse offices of famous designers, and he almost got beaten up in a downtown alley, searching for the entrance to a tiny, off-off-off-off Broadway theater.

Waiting for his next assignment, Max sat around the SAB lobby joking with his pals and flirting with the girls. His mother detested his having the job, and she got frantic thinking about his wandering around the city. She liked knowing (or at least thinking she knew) just where her son was during the day. Max never told her about the scary times, the time in the alley or the scariest of all, the day he was on his way to the Waldorf-Astoria. He was walking down Park Avenue, not far from the hotel, when suddenly there were shouts on the median that divides the avenue. Some tourists were hurling racial slurs at a black messenger whose bicycle had brushed them, calling him a nigger and saying that he would be in trouble where they came from. Enraged, the messenger reached into his satchel, pulled out a pistol, and told the tourists it would be a good idea if they got their white asses out of town. Max was about twenty feet away. He hit the pavement and hid behind a potted plant, on his belly. The tourists fled; the messenger put away his gun and went about his business, and Max went on to make his delivery too. He could hardly walk, his knees were so weak, but eventually he calmed down. His mother never knew.

Often Max rushed between the theater and the school. That was the best; that was when he got to go in the stage entrance, and that was when he got to see all the dancers and imagine what it was like to be one of them. He liked that, and he also liked earning fifty dollars a week. His mother didn't mind that part, either. Max got paid every Friday; often his cash was the family's only spending money for the weekend.

Alex and Rob and Peter and Drew were all now in Advanced Men's every morning. Their classes were over at two o'clock in the afternoon. All but one of Max's friends had made it into Advanced, and his enemy Josh was promoted, too. Brandon was the only chum still in Intermediate with Max, but he was at school in the suburbs all day long. Brandon lives in Scarsdale, New York, a wealthy suburb of the city. He started his dance lessons with Jacques d'Amboise. His parents are together, and his father is a successful businessman; his is a "normal" nuclear household, and his support systems are in place. Brandon needs to grow taller; he doesn't have the best feet for dancing, and he can't always make them do exactly what he wants them to, but he can jump with the lightness of a soufflé. Brandon's folks like the idea that he dances, but they worry about his future. They want him to be happy; they also want him to be comfortable financially. They're not convinced ballet will provide properly for him. Brandon takes every class seriously; he listens hard and tries hard. He's made a deal with his parents: If he doesn't get hired by some ballet company within one year after he graduates from high school, he will go to college. A pact with the devil couldn't weigh more heavily on his intentions. He doesn't want to go to college; he wants to dance, and if he has anything to do with it, if he can control it at all, he will.

Intermediate class meets at five-thirty P.M. so that the middle-level and generally mid-teen boys can still have a full day of regular school. Max was in neither regular school nor

Advanced class, but his workday ended just as his pals were
finishing with Stanley or Krammie, so they all went to lunch
together. Max listened to them talk about what Krammie did
that morning or whether they thought Stanley knew they
were alive, and pretended that he was really of them, with
them, on their level. It was only later in the day, when he was
in class with the younger boys, that Max admitted to himself
how far apart he felt from his friends, how far behind, how
much lesser! To his brothers and sisters he always bragged
about being in charge in Intermediate, about how he had
been there for so long that he was the only one with a special,
reserved place at the barre, and about how none of the others
would dare try to take his spot. Then he would remember his
first months in class, when he was new and young and little
and encased in baby fat. The older boys liked the plucky little
Texan; they called him the Pillsbury Doughboy, and they
regularly picked him up and stuffed him in the small closet in
the studio. He would squeal and squirm delightedly; all their
fun would be enhanced by impending danger, by the possibility of being discovered roughhousing by Mr. Rapp. It seemed
a century ago to Max. Says he, "It's such a waste. I sit around
all day, just waiting for class, and then when it's finally time, I
don't want to be there."

Two o'clock means lunchtime. The boys are always
starving. No one in the group ever has superfluous spendable
cash, so they all know where they can find the best food deal.
They are noted authorities on that student standby, pizza by
the slice. New York City fairly teems with purveyors of pizza;
small, semi-clean shops usually run by Greeks or Arabs,
seldom by Italians. For under two dollars a lunch of one
steamy, gooey, slice of tomato-and-cheese pizza and a diet
soft drink can replenish what energy the boys spent in class or

what Max lost delivering messages all over town. They know every possible pizza parlor within walking distance, and they have different favorites for different purposes: one offers maybe not the very best pizza but certainly the very biggest slices; another is the chic parlor of choice, one where PCS girls eat; still a third has the best food but is small and often crowded.

Brothers, brothers-in-law, and male cousins work side by side in these shops, chattering away loudly to each other in tongues few of their customers can decipher, usually to the accompaniment of loud, exotic music blasting from a portable radio. Often one of the relatives is in the window, kneading the pizza dough and twirling it around with style. Plates and napkins are paper; glasses and cutlery, if used, are plastic. Customers are rushed through the line in a scene worthy of *Saturday Night Live*; cans of soda are slapped down on the counter; slices slid onto trays; money always handled by the same fingers that serve the food. The whole process—getting a trayful, finding a table, and gobbling down the hot, greasy food—can be accomplished in about twenty minutes.

Then it's back to Sixty-sixth Street and up to the Juilliard cafeteria and student lounge. SAB has no facilities of its own, but its landlord, the Juilliard School, permits the tenant's students to share in its modest accommodations for food and relaxation. This is where Max shines. The goal is to be surrounded by as many friends as possible; numbers count. Max gets *A*'s in cafeteria. He sits back, lights a cigarette— currently he favors Lucky Strikes, the old, unfiltered Lucky Strikes, mostly because no one mooches them—and holds court. The cast of characters swells and shrinks organically as boys and girls join, sip a cup of coffee, smoke a cigarette (they don't eat here, except for the occasional yogurt), and go about their pursuits. Parties are planned on these premises, pairings paired, and peer prestige pursued. As Max says, "All I know about Josh and me is: Who's always surrounded in the cafeteria, and who's always sitting alone?"

The social alignment at SAB greatly favors the boys. There are many more beautiful bunheads than there are available danseurs, and lots of the girls are eager for romance. Usually they give the parties; the boys arrive in flocks, unless they have a steady. Andrew, for instance, is seeing Margaret exclusively; the two are rarely apart. Margaret has brought religion as well as romance to Andrew's life; they go to church together, and Bible study groups too. Margaret is not very popular—she's a bit holier-than-thou (or thou or thou)—but she is an extraordinary dancer. Andrew, who used to be the Wild One, Max's idol, is popular with one and all. He's having a terrible time with his dancing. His body has betrayed him completely; he is always injured. Drew has taken very few whole classes in the last couple of years, mostly having to stop after the barre to avoid further abusing his mangled legs, knees, and hips. He's already graduated from PCS; his professor father is urging him to go to college, and Andrew is even starting to think that's not a bad idea. But not yet. He can't give up just yet.

Margaret has been Andrew's salvation in this world, even as she works for the same for him in the next. He was depressed; he was turning into an all-pro hanger-around. He just couldn't watch class day after day, never being able to join in. It was too hard. So he'd stay home, watch television, fiddle with a video game joystick, and do little else. Max joined him in the pursuit of nothing many a day, and the two sat around drinking beer and competing in role-playing games. Now Drew is working for a photographer and seeing

Margaret instead of Max. He's a whole new person, and Max doesn't like it. Max is jealous. "I don't know about Drew," he says. "It's as though he figures he's eighteen now, and he has to grow up suddenly. And that Margaret. She just doesn't like me."

Says Andrew, "Max doesn't understand; I'd rather be with Margaret than anyone else."

Other friends of Max's peel off from the cafeteria group for a variety of reasons: Alex is usually off to some commercial audition. He's already done one and he's eager for more. Ilan is a movie actor, so he has to see his agent and read for parts, etc. Peter and Rob do lecture/demonstrations for Suki Shorer. She puts on programs in schools to show what ballet is all about. It's great for the demonstrators. The school audiences are usually very enthusiastic, plus the SAB kids get invaluable performing experience and equally invaluable performing pay. It's also an honor to be asked. As usual, only the top kids get chosen. Peter and Rob are among the best.

Friday nights are party nights for SAB kids. On Friday nights dancers become "normal" teenagers. They don't look like others their age: They have those duckling feet and much better posture as a rule; they're better-looking and more inventively dressed, and their conversations are more about tendu than trig. But on Friday nights they let loose just like their counterparts in all fifty states. The parties are usually held in apartments shared by groups of girls; there is much drink but little food. These girls have intense relationships with food, but usually it is one based on fantasy, desire, and sacrifice. They think about, talk about, and dream about food instead of eating it as they would like to. The boys bring beer to the parties, and the hostesses mix up a batch of "jungle juice." These are kids, remember. They drink the way teenagers drink—foolishly and to get drunk. (Not to say that plenty of adult martini drinkers are not similarly motivated.) The recipe for jungle juice is: Take whatever alcohol you can get your hands on. Clean out the liquor cabinet if there is one. If not, gather a collection of it-matters-not-what. Mix. Chill. Drink.

There are problem drinkers among these students, just as there are in epidemic proportions all around America. There are drug users, too, and lots of dope smokers. These are kids who labor long and hard all week; who must take with grace and intelligence constant criticism and correction; who live public, precarious existences; and who have intense feelings about what they are doing. Many are away from home at a very tender age, without the support of caring parents and interested brothers and sisters. They are kids who flirt with danger and injury daily, who are constantly assessed and reassessed, and who constantly assess and reassess themselves in that ever-present harsh mirror. They are kids who live for an approving smile from the teacher, who get heady with joy over a good class or a combination of newly learned steps. It's hard. Some turn regularly to chemistry for help. Some of the boys smoke pot just before class, thinking it helps them relax and do better. Mr. Rapp says that he spots them instantly and that he disagrees that a toke helps tours. "You see that vacant look," he says. "Then you hear, 'That's soooo beautiful, that step.' I hate drugs!" Most of these kids, though, just blow off steam on Friday nights. In style. The music blares, the dancing beats any school dance you've ever seen, and the kids are as high as kites—some even naturally.

Couples fall loosely into place. Ann and Ilan have been going together for months; they're the most established twosome. Alex and Claudia are drifting toward each other, and so are Max and another Ann. After a bit, they wander out into the hallway; they sit on the steps and kiss and fumble. Says Max, "Ann and I dance together in adagio. There's always been this natural attraction. That night I needed a massage, and then one thing led to another." SAB Friday-night parties often don't end. Everybody just poops out. Then mattresses are assembled, lined up together on the floor, and the kids pile on. They all sleep together like a giant teenage sandwich, everybody hugging and snoozing and touching. Max never stays overnight. His mother insists he be home. Besides, his Saturday-morning class is early, at nine-thirty; the Advanced Men's doesn't meet until half past noon.

XIII.

Princes

October brings more to the ballet world than autumn leaves and the need for leg warmers. All over America, October ushers in the start of the *Nutcracker* season. For dancers that means work. Days shorten and cool off; kids start to listen to tales of that odd Herr Drosslemeyer and his nephew; bookstore windows fill up with the latest variations on this popular theme. "The Waltz of the Flowers" sneaks onto the pop-tune charts. By November, it will be accompanied by a bullet, the symbol of galloping popularity. Ballet schools hold auditions for the children's parts, and companies select Cavaliers and Sugar Plums. Casts are assembled and rehearsals begun.

For professional male dancers *Nutcracker* time is bonanza time, guest appearance time. Experienced Cavaliers command tidy sums for one night or one week of guest appearances. Some dart about the country, making several guest shots each year.

Bill DeGregory is one of the top danseurs with the Pennsylvania Ballet. Bill is a well-endowed technician and an extraordinary partner. His company performs a lot less often than the New York City Ballet or ABT, however, and dancers don't get paid for the weeks they don't dance. So Bill makes *Nutcracker* guest appearances as regularly as he can, often with his wife, ballerina Tamara Hadley. Guesting gives Bill financial stability, and he doesn't mind all the travel. In fact, he enjoys it. He wouldn't change places with anyone; he wouldn't join the NYCB for anything. He's been with the Pennsylvania Ballet for his entire career, and he intends to keep it that way. He grew up on a small farm in New Hampshire, one of ten children— all of whom were adopted. He got his training in Champaign, Illinois, and came to New York when he graduated, to audition for American Ballet Theatre. After one class at ABT and one at SAB, he fled. He wanted no part of either. The competitive tension that he felt in both places gave him the creeps; it had nothing to do with what he wanted out of life. So Bill hightailed it to Philadelphia, just in time for the Pennsylvania Ballet's auditions. As soon as he walked in the door, he felt as though he had arrived home. In fact, he had.

Sean Lavery lives the pressurized life of a City Ballet dancer. He dances any number of Cavaliers with his own company every Christmas, and he also manages to fit in at least one gig—in Detroit. He says, "I'm trying to fix up my apartment, and I think 'Another week in Detroit, another payment on a new kitchen.' "

Nuts season is frantic for student dancers as well; it's their time to live like the pros; to audition, rehearse, and perform; to get a glimpse into their futures. Well-connected older student princes occasionally make guest appearances themselves for fun and profit. Peter Martins has arranged for his son Nilas and Nilas's chum Gordon to dance in *Nuts* in Caracas, Venezuela. Other teenagers are often offered parts by small American companies that can't afford the higher-priced pros.

October arrived, and Max decided it was his turn, that he was going to get a chance to dance and to earn some money for it. So he talked to Leslie Otto and got her to hire him for her production with the Mid-Atlantic Ballet. It wouldn't be City Ballet; it wouldn't be Caracas; he wouldn't be the Cavalier, either; but it was *Nutcracker*, and it was a job.

The Mid-Atlantic Ballet is the performing company that Leslie Otto started to go with her school in suburban Bronxville, New York. Every year Mid-Atlantic puts on a homegrown version of *Nuts* that is basically Balanchinian. That is, Leslie starts out with Mr. B.'s *Nutcracker* and then adapts it to her needs. Some steps are simplified, and some variations are eliminated altogether to accommodate the dancers she has at the moment. Costumes are sewn by parents, sets are made of plaster of paris and spit, and some of Leslie's ballerinas go on stage sporting a little extra avoirdupois and the occasional stick of chewing gum. Still, Mid-Atlantic manages to put on a thoroughly enjoyable show every Christmas, one that is magically transformed into a recognizable facsimile of the *Nutcracker* that plays the State Theater.

Like every other ballet school director, Leslie is usually able to gather a pretty ballerina or two, but also like every other ballet school director, she must import some of her danseurs. Unlike the others, though, Leslie has some special resources to call upon. Her daughter, Debbie, is an SAB student, so there are those boys, like Max, to choose from. And she has another advantage as well. Three sons. All three of her oldest boys—she has seven children in all—are professional ballet dancers. Bill and David Otto are with the New York City Ballet, and Phil was with Milwaukee until a broken foot sent him home for a spell. The spell happened to coincide with *Nutcracker* season, so Phil was pressed into immediate service—broken foot or no broken foot.

Leslie Otto is a 5'3" bundle of grit, hyperactivity, and ambition. That she takes on doing an elaborate *Nutcracker* is proof enough of her bravery and optimistic spirit ("Either that," she says, "or proof that I'm crazy"), but further proof is that she stages a couple of other large-scale ballets every year as well. In her spare time she runs her school and raises her brood, who range in age from four to thirty. Her boys are all big and strong; she's tiny, but she's tougher than all of them put together. "Sometimes," she says, "when I need one of them and I tell him to get out here, that I need help with a part or with painting a room, he'll say, 'Oh, Mom, I'm a New York City Ballet dancer now.' I say, 'I don't care what you are, you get out here and help your mother.' " The next train usually delivers an Otto, dancing slippers or paintbrush in hand.

Bryant Young is another man Leslie Otto can count on. He appears in all her productions. Bryant is an SAB graduate who works full-time for Jim Henson on that TV avenue known as *Sesame Street*. Bryant is Snuffleupagus, the huge, gentle, lumbering pachydermlike friend of Big Bird. Inside the gigantic, loved-by-little-ones-everywhere Snuffy is the compact, fast-moving, and nervous Bryant. He helps Leslie in a number of ways. He dances for her, he helps her redo the choreography, and he also conducts rehearsals. In a professional company Bryant would be called the régisseur.

For the first of Leslie's five *Nutcracker* performances Bryant can't get away from being Snuffy, so Max will dance his parts. That gives Max a lot to learn in a short time; he has his own two parts—Spanish and Hoops—and now he's got

Bryant's as well—Chinese and Wooden Soldier. He didn't realize just what he would be getting himself into. Bryant and Max have arranged to meet, just the two of them. The rest of the rehearsals are being held up in Westchester on the weekends; this is an added "emergency call" so that Bryant can teach Max what he needs to know.

Bryant dashes into the studio where he and Max will work. Max has been waiting. Bryant is late, rushing and checking his watch like a Hollywood mogul ready to take a meeting. "I've only got forty-five minutes, so let's get going," he barks, all business. Max tries to seem laid back and attempts a few feeble jokes. Bryant is having none of it. He wants to show Max the rather difficult steps quickly; he wants Max to get them down fast or not at all, and he wants to be on his way. No dancer likes teaching another his part. Bryant goes quickly through the solo, marking the steps, walking through them. Max is confused and intimidated; he'd like things to slow down. Bryant has no intention of babying his replacement; he'd rather not be sharing, anyhow. Bryant is firm about not changing some jumps that Max finds very difficult, and he ignores Max's pleas for "Seeses. Let's put seeses in there. I'm great at seeses." (*Seeses* is Americanized colloquial for entrechat sixes, where the male springs up into the air from fifth position and his feet crisscross three full times before he lands back on earth in fifth position. They're hard to do.) Max *is* great at seeses; he does them very well and seemingly without effort. Bryant couldn't care less. Soon Bryant says, "Now the coda goes like this," to which Max replies, "The what?" Bryant shakes his head in disbelief. His interest in this task and his patience with Max are running very short. Soon the allotted time is up and Bryant is gone. Max is winded. He sits down, scratches his head, and wonders how on earth he's going to pull it all off.

Mid-Atlantic's girls rehearse for *Nutcracker* every day after school, with taped music and a videotape of the previous year's performance as a guide. The boys come out from the city every Sunday at first, then Saturdays and Sundays. Max often oversleeps and is awakened by a call from Leslie, who then has to wait a couple of hours for her Spaniard to speed out on the train. Another SAB'er is also in Leslie's *Nuts*; he never oversleeps. Ben Huys is from Belgium. He's at SAB because he won a year's scholarship at an international ballet contest. To come here Ben turned down job offers from seven European companies. He is not sure he made the right decision.

Ben is Leslie's Cavalier, except for one variation, which son Phil will dance. Ben is tall, gifted, and regal, a *danseur noble* in the making. He has amazing feet with huge arches—perfect dancer's feet. His back is strong and straight, his mind quick and alert. Ben is even more used to special treatment than Max and his friends. He has always been a very special dancer. He is also the son of a doctor and has had a life blessed with high status, loving parents, talent and brains, and many things material. Now Ben is in New York, far away from his famly, with no one clucking over him. He is living simply too. He has few friends; he can't understand what Stanley wants in his class, and he's having a hard time adjusting to the SAB way. He wants more classes, and he wants them to be more the way they were in Brussels. Mostly he wants to go home. Ben is miserable, lonesome, homesick, but he's always on time for rehearsals; he works hard, never cracking jokes or slouching around or teasing his partner. Max is late, slouchy, and always joking. But Ben can't do seeses; that makes Max feel great.

Max and Ben are not friends. One would be hard-pressed, in fact, to say that they are friendly. Riding out to

177

rehearsals in the same car, they exchange the briefest of greetings and direct any subsequent conversation to others. They don't chat at breaks; neither ever asks the other a question or offers a comment. Both say the other is cold. Both are correct.

Rehearsals fly by, and suddenly it's show time. An old show-biz adage says that a terrible dress rehearsal ensures a good performance. Leslie Otto hopes the saying holds true; Mid-Atlantic's *Nutcracker* dress rehearsal is a mess. Nothing goes right. No one seems to know the steps properly, the lights won't work, and some of the sets are unfinished. Costumes rip, tempers fray, and the misery goes on until well after midnight. The first performance is a matinee scheduled for the next day. It's a special show just for school kids, busloads and busloads of school kids. They invade the theater, running, giggling, chattering. Most are about to have their first experience with classical dance. *The Nutcracker* is about to weave its spell. As soon as the music starts, the kids quiet down, and they sit spellbound through the whole ballet, with only occasional *ooooo*hs or *aaaaa*hs breaking the silence. This is the warmest, most available group of first-nighters (actually first-afternooners) possible. Wild applause follows every solo, and at the end the filled theater throbs with excited children clapping madly until their hands hurt.

Backstage, before the performance, things got a bit hairy. Leslie was nervous; she had a cold and a fever, and her frayed edges were beginning to show. Max tried to stay out of her way so he wouldn't get snapped at. Little ones darted about, with parents in hot pursuit, trying to capture and costume their mini-angels. Stitches had to be taken here, curls combed there, and emergency safety pins were always in demand. A portable barre was set up so that the older dancers

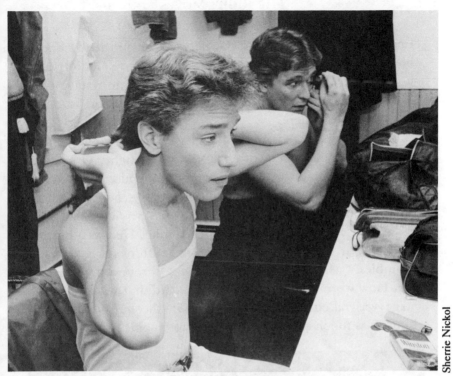

The roar of the greasepaint, five minutes to curtain.

could warm up. Stagehands ran through set changes one final time, repeated cues again and again. Teenage ballerinas pinned their glistening hair up in topknots and clipped sparkling "gems" to their ears. The little girls were ruddy with excitement, making makeup redundant. The boys—Phil Otto, Ben, and Max—were all crammed into a tiny dressing room that would get even more snug when Bryant joined them the following day. At the last minute Max couldn't find the black tights for one of his costumes or the white ones for another. He was frantic. Finally he borrowed some from Phil, a neat trick since Phil is a full foot taller. They all dipped into

Phil's makeup kit, but no one besides the pro really knew how to apply the stuff. Ten minutes! Oh, my God! It had been a long time since Max had been out on a stage; his stomach churned. Ben sat calmly, reading, just a little bit apart from the others.

The first act started, the party scene. Max did his bit very well, as the parent of a six-year-old naughty Otto boy. He walked around the stage elegantly, mimed conversations as though he were a happy guest, then scooped up his mischievous "son" and exited left. After a quick change of costume it was back on as a wooden soldier. He was a bit too wooden but otherwise okay. Backstage afterward, he was a shambles. "M*aaa*n," he said, moaning, "I screwed up badly. . . . How were the seeses? M*aaannnn*. I didn't warm up; the stage was raked . . ." A long look in the mirror, then, to himself as much as anyone else, "Always some excuse."

Party scene antics with Ben and Max and a little Otto.

Sherrie Nickol

180

The second act was a bit chaotic and filled with rough edges, but everyone got through it. Max pulled off his two solos and put seeses in where Bryant had insisted he do jumps. Ben was princely, assured, graceful, and strong. Phil Otto was massive and gave no indication whatever that he was dancing with a broken bone. Then everyone got to bask in the stomping and whistling of the kid-filled audience.

Max's mother came to the matinee that Thursday, and every other performance as well. She never missed one of Max's performances.

For the Thursday matinee, the school performance, Brenda appeared with a friend who was visiting from Florida; they came out to Tarrytown in his car. Brenda looked like a fashion plate, an antique shawl wrapped around the shoulders of her cloth coat, her hair totally in place, makeup and jewelry on, as well as high heels and stockings. Her walk was a little grand, and she was excellent at shawl swooping. Backstage she swooped to congratulate her son, who beamed. She agreed to take both Ben and Max back to Manhattan but then was unable somehow to find room for Ben. The cavalier had to walk to the railroad station and take the train back. Max rode in luxury.

By the Saturday matinee most of the production's kinks had been ironed out. Nerves were overcome, and the whole show looked better, more cohesive. Leslie was more tired than ever but happy, proud of herself and everyone else. She festooned the dressing rooms with flowers; all the dancers felt like stars. There were two Saturday performances, and then a final *Nutcracker* on Sunday. Phil Otto wanted to include a City Ballet tradition in his mother's *Nutcracker*. The New Year's Eve performance at the State Theater, the last of a whole month of *Nutcracker*s, gets a bit zany. Dancers change roles, play pranks on each other, and misappropriate parts of costumes. Phil planned for a surprise appearance by his brother Bill, and he and Max concocted women's costumes for themselves for the party scene. Phil also wanted a boisterous, roistering party after the Saturday night performance. Max couldn't wait.

While Max was dancing in *Nutcracker* his mother sold their apartment and moved the family into the Hotel Empire—where Charlie lives. She'd been a wreck worrying the sale through; it looked iffy for a while, and she badly needed the money. Now she wouldn't have to scratch quite so much for at least a year. She hadn't felt confident enough of the sale to commit to another place, though, and she couldn't face unpacking all the stuff she'd had to pack all by herself, anyhow. So it was the Hotel Empire for the gypsy-esque Fuquas. No sooner were they in than she checked them out, however.

Since Max's performances were out in the suburbs, and since she intended to see each one, she saw no logic in paying for a hotel room in New York. Brenda the sister moved in with a friend for the weekend, and Brenda the mother and Max stayed with other friends near Tarrytown. After the Saturday matinee Max's mother came backstage again, not swooping this time, and not chic, either. She was in jeans and an old shirt, with no makeup on and hair that could have used a brush. She looked done in, harried, which indeed she was. Max told her he would be going with Phil after the evening performance, and she told Max that he would be doing no such thing. Also, she told him, she wanted some cash, would he please give her some. The cast had been paid, she thought, and she wanted Max to give her some of his salary. He went into his dressing room and closed the door. She shouted her request in through the barrier, and he shouted back, in an embarrassed, little-boy voice, "Honest, Mutti, I don't have any." She shrugged and left.

Saturday night's performance was the best. All the dancers were experienced, confident, and loose; their adrenaline was running high. The audience was filled with families, and they all loved Mid-Atlantic's *Nuts*. Afterward Max went off with his mother; Phil Otto had to have his party without the party-loving Texan. On Sunday brother Bill surprised his mom, and Phil's other tricks came off too. There is a point in the proceedings when a stuffed mouse is tossed onstage and the female party guests shriek in fear. The littlest Otto, dressed in brown fuzz, ran out instead, to the delight of everyone, including Leslie, and Phil himself made a startling

The dancer's bonus: applause and bows.

Sherrie Nickol

appearance as the world's tallest female party guest. When it was all over, Max returned to the Empire with his mother, and Phil limped on home with his parents. The youngest of the three dancing Ottos spent the next eight weeks in a cast.

When they were very young, Leslie Otto taught her boys ballet basics and then sent them off to her own alma mater, SAB. "I remember when I was only tiny and she was teaching in my grandmother's basement," recalls Phil. "David and I hid behind our grandfather's desk so we wouldn't have to go down there. Mother found us, ripped us out, and plunked us in that class. She used to dress me in little red tights and stick Dippity-Do on my hair," continues the huge danseur. "I hated it . . . but it did get me a starring part in the City Ballet's *Nutcracker*." His brothers may have jobs with the NYCB, but Phil is the only Otto to have been a *Nutcracker* prince with the company. "You must understand," he says in all seriousness at age twenty-three, "I really thought I *was* the prince. I wouldn't even wash the dishes at home because princes don't wash dishes."

When ballet companies go on tour, they often stage big, romantic, popular works, many of which require children. It's impossible to travel with a full complement of little people, though, so ballet schools in the host cities offer their students to the guests. The Ballet Russe did this for years all over the United States; even Maureen Reagan, Ronald's daughter, was cast in one Los Angeles *Nutcracker*. When the Otto boys were little, companies from Europe were always visiting New York, and the three were much in demand. They sang with the Metropolitan Opera children's chorus, too, so they were regularly onstage at the Met, and they were also often written up in newspapers and featured on television.

Those were heady days for the three sons of a suburban truck driver. Their friends were green with jealousy, and a long opera sometimes meant they weren't home and in their Dr. Dentons until well after midnight. The best parts, though, their favorite times, were with the touring ballet companies. The Ottos danced with England's Royal Ballet, with Germany's Stuttgart, and even with the U.S.S.R.'s Bolshoi. Phil says that those appearances were what really made them want to be dancers, what made them aspire to princeship. Like so many others their age, the Ottos saw Nureyev dance and were awestruck. They were luckier than most, however; they didn't see the Russian superstar on television or from the audience. They were onstage with him, and they even got to talk to him backstage, to hang around his dressing room a little. The Ottos were swept away. Who wouldn't be?

And then there's Mom. Leslie Otto takes no prisoners. Ballet is her life, and she was determined that it be her sons' lives too. The boys were going to dance, and that was that. Says Phil, "Our mother basically ruled us. We got vibes of what she thought was important—ballet and opera, not high school. I never even finished high school. We've never talked about it, but I always felt that Dad wanted some regular sons—whatever regular is. I, we, all wanted to be regular. You know, go fishing and stuff. Dad's a pussycat actually, though, and he never really tried to stop us from dancing. Sometimes I wished he had, like the year I wanted to ice-skate and go to hockey camp. I begged Mother and begged her and begged her, but she won. It was dancing instead of skating."

The Otto boys were all offered scholarships to study in London, at the Royal Ballet school, but Mom wanted them closer to home. So SAB it was. It wasn't easy for any of them.

David was bounced out more than half a dozen times, "twice by Mr. Balanchine himself," as he brags, and at least once for "fooling around" with a girl on the staircase. Bill was told he would never make it, that his neck was too short. Phil became a casualty of adolescence. He grew and grew and grew, upward and outward. He got too tall and he got too fat. "At fourteen," he says, "my life really crashed in around me. I was so miserable that I barely went out of my room for a couple of years. I really mean it when I said I thought I was a prince, and then suddenly there I was, big and fat. Nothing helped. I ate ten candy bars a day, and sometimes I would even steal them. Talk about a kid in trouble. My parents took me twice to a shrink, but I wouldn't go back."

Phil credits Richard Thomas, Sean Lavery's teacher, with keeping him and his brother dancing post-SAB. "I still consider him one of my best friends," says Phil. "He believed in us." Bill Otto danced with several other companies before joining the NYCB and proving his early teachers wrong. He was twenty-five when he got accepted; he holds the record for oldest corps member ever hired. He did make it, though, and Phil hasn't yet given up hopes of joining his brothers in the Balanchinian fraternity. It's his fondest wish, for Phil quite literally dreams about dancing on the stage of the State Theater. "I had it again just the other night," he says, "my *Nutcracker* dream. It was my last performance. I was the prince, and they were giving me my nutcracker. I worked with it, and then it was all over. I woke up with tears streaming down my face. Isn't that sad? And I thought I had put it all behind me."

The eight weeks Phil sat around with his foot in a cast were torture, but there is one thing—only one—that is worse for a dancer than sitting immobilized: the awful reality when the cast is taken off. Muscles shrink, waistlines grow, and strength vanishes. Getting back into shape takes a superhuman discipline, but dancers develop superhuman discipline. Getting back into shape also takes a patience, a trust, and a confidence that nothing in a dancer's experience has ever helped him develop. He must find them on his own somehow. He must banish fear and control overeagerness. Coming back too fast, being impatient, almost always results in reinjury or a new injury and a further delay. The injured danseur is supposed to trust time, usually his enemy, and go slowly, with confidence that he will get back to his dancing weight, strength, and suppleness better if he rebuilds carefully, sure all the while he is healing that no one else will catch the director's eye and take over his parts, position, and place. It's impossible. Someone will take over; there are plenty who are able and eager, and even the greatest of the great are not indispensable. So, dancers dance hurt even more than athletes play hurt. "Balanchine used to say, 'You don't dance for your health.' " says Larry Matthews. Many dancers lose their health through dance, often without regret.

XIV.

Pain

The relationship dancers have with injury is much like that which a cat maintains with water. They fear and dread torn ligaments, broken bones, and arthritic hips all the while they flirt with them, court them. All their magic-making invites disaster. Everything a dancer does puts him in jeopardy. Performing is a risk, partnering is treacherous, even class is potentially harmful. No ballet movement is the way nature intended. That's the point; ballet improves on nature. Ballet movements are more than mere natural movements: more beautiful, more elegant, more extreme, and more visible. More dangerous too.

Turnout, the open stance that must become second nature to all dancers, the position that shows off their legs and the steps they are doing to the fullest advantage, is treacherous to their bodies. Turnout is not just walking like a duck; it's not just in the feet. Turnout starts in the hips and works its way down, taking a huge, stressful toll on the joint where it originates and all the muscles and tendons along its route. Ankles and knees, not to mention toes, get assaulted constantly, too, and a male dancer's back crunches its way through every ballet. There is no careful bending of the

188

knees to help distribute the strain, no artless use of body mechanics to ease the pain. Lifts must be done artfully, beautifully, in a way that increases the stress and strain. His arms must be extended, his back straight, his knees un-curved. She must be held high above his head, or on one shoulder, or right out in front, or to one side, or in a number of other poses that make spines snap, crackle, and pop like a whole carton of cereal. Even the tiniest ballerina weighs enough to tax her partner's anatomy in those positions; and many are not tiny at all.

Alexandra Danilova is diminutive, but in a *Ballet Review* commemoration of Anton Dolin, she tells a story about their first meeting. He was to become her partner. They greeted each other politely, and then Dolin took a long look at Danilova and said, "You know what? I'm a dancer, not a piano mover. Get thin." Danilova promptly dieted away her few extra pounds. Dolin was an international star then; he could make such a demand.

Phil Otto is not a star, national or international. Says he, "When you dance with a company, you have to catch what they throw at you. And when you're big like I am, they throw anything at you. Sometimes I feel as though what I really am is just a forklift."

SAB dancers don't have bodybuilding classes; they must develop the strengths that will best help them avoid injury on their own. Some go to specialists; others try to work by themselves. Some do as many as two hundred sit-ups a day to strengthen their back-supporting stomach muscles. Jac-ques d'Amboise advised his son Chris to practice lifting the heavy sandbags that are found backstage, to hold them in front of him and move them from side to side to build the muscles he would need for lifting ballerinas.

Pounding takes a terrific toll, too, on young bodies, and older ones as well. Max's hip problem, a cyst, was due to years of turning out and jumping and landing and leaping, although he claims it was a direct result of his being forced to hurl himself out a second-story window after his older brothers somehow managed to lock him inside their Dallas house.

When Sean Lavery was fifteen, doctors discovered a cyst on his knee but decided not to operate in hopes that he would grow out of it. He didn't, and after seven more years of abuse the knee was, he says, "a cumulative mess." That was March 1980. The New York City Ballet was preparing for its spring season; rehearsing, making new ballets. One new work, *Ballade*, was to feature Lavery and Merrill Ashley; George Balanchine was the choreographer. Lavery worked and rehearsed, and his knee got worse daily. Finally he had no choice but to go under the microsurgical knife. His kneecap was in the wrong place, and inside, said his doctors, it "looked like crabmeat." *Ballade* was to premier in May; Lavery was determined to dance that first performance. He was going to get on that stage and whistle down the wind. "I was like Chester on *Gunsmoke*," he says, "dragging that thin, weak leg behind me." He gulped down four Indocin (an anti-inflammatory) a day and kept saying he could do it, he really could. He did Nautilus and tried every other sort of muscle-building machine or technique; you name it, he did it. Nothing worked. Eventually he had to admit defeat, and he had to teach all that had been done on *Ballade* to Ib Andersen, who would dance the premiere, whose ballet it would become. It was a nightmare. "I thought Mr. Balanchine would never look at me again," says Lavery, remembering his misery. He couldn't do *Ballade*, but he insisted on dancing some of the easier parts all season, and toward the end he did a few of the tougher ones as well. "My knee looked like a pork roast," he says. "It took me a full year to feel like I had a knee again, and I was dancing the whole time."

Freud's dictum that "there are no accidents" may be a bit too severe, but all dancers are acutely aware of the tangled ties between emotion and injury. All agree that hurts are often at least partially self-inflicted. Sometimes a too-soon promotion to the next rank will cause a back to go out in a subconscious attack of fear of success, and other times anger and disgruntlement at not going ahead fast enough will invite pulls and tears. An unhappy love life, a dying parent, or just plain free-floating anxiety can cause sprains or spasms. A tense body is in more jeopardy than a relaxed one. When the twenty-year-old Jock Soto became the youngest male to attain the rank of NYCB principal dancer since Jacques d'Amboise some three decades earlier, Soto's back promptly clutched and wouldn't unclutch, keeping him off the stage for the remainder of that season. Knotted-up intestines with no disease sent Chris d'Amboise to the hospital twice.

Peter Frame is a soloist with the City Ballet; his twin brother, Paul, is in the company's corps. Both have had their battles with competition, separation, and injury. It's complicated being a twin; it's complicated being the son of a minister; it's complicated being a ballet dancer. The Frame brothers have had to come to grips with all three while continuing to perform at the level expected of all City Ballet members. Peter came to New York (from West Virginia) first; Paul tried college, then followed. When his twin joined him, Peter felt halved. "I had come to New York; I had made friends and made a place for myself. Three years later Paul came, and suddenly my friends didn't quite know who I was." One short month after Peter joined the company he tore two ligaments in his left foot. It happened right in company class; Mr. Balanchine was teaching. Peter landed after an airborne move, and the whole studio could hear the ripping and crunching. The other dancers were frozen with fear. They knew it was bad, and they knew it could have been any one of them. Peter walked out of the room quietly, as though nothing were wrong. Says he, "Every new company member goes through a different ordeal. I wanted to do everything right so badly. . . . Mr. Balanchine said to me afterward, 'Dear, you must think about it. It takes years. It's nothing that you can do overnight.' "

Five years later Peter tore ligaments in his right foot, and broke it as well. Shaking his head and shrugging his shoulders, he explains: "We'd been on a gruelling tour. It was exhausting. I was getting soloist parts, and I was still in the corps. I was just not ready. I was not clear; I got scared. First I lost fifteen pounds, and then I broke my foot—right on-stage—and fainted. And you know what? It was a relief to wake up in the hospital. I took six and a half months off. For two months I just slept twelve hours a day, every day. Then I went home to West Virginia and was a hick for a couple of months. I fished and fished and fished through all my garbage, and I got back to being a normal person. I also got reinspired. I got myself ready to become a soloist. Then, when it came, I was ready. It was the right time then, and I was able to reap what I had sown."

Sean Lavery is well acquainted with the toll that emotion, stress, and tension can take on a dancer's body. Lavery grew up realizing that it was possible for him to please those close to him, that he could make them all happy if he just worked hard enough at it. What he didn't realize, couldn't realize, was the toll all that pleasing took on him. All he could see were the rewards, the approval, he got for his efforts. He did, after all, soar to the top at City Ballet faster than any other male ever.

Lavery never says no. Unlike many of his colleagues, he has never refused to dance, and some evenings he does impossibly different and difficult pieces back to back. No other City Ballet male could or would do the same.

In the fall of 1983, before their New York season, the NYCB went on a European tour that took them to London, Copenhagen, and Paris. The dancers arrived in London on a Saturday, rehearsed on Sunday, and opened on Monday, jet lag or no jet lag. Lavery performed on opening night and on every night thereafter. He was overworked and overwrought, overtired and over-nervous. His back hurt like hell. After a while he wasn't able to eat. Then his right arm started to go numb. He tried to ignore it but it got worse. Soon he didn't even have the strength to turn on a faucet. Still he danced. The last matinee of their run he danced *Symphony in C*, a big, classical Balanchine ballet. By that evening, "I couldn't stand up," he says. "I couldn't breathe. I felt nervous, crazy. I thought, 'I'll walk it off,' but by eleven o'clock that night I literally couldn't walk.

"Friends brought me muscle relaxers and Valium, which I took. Then I lay down on the floor on my side. Finally I fell asleep at four in the morning, and I awoke at six-thirty. I still couldn't walk, and we were leaving for Denmark on a chartered plane. With each arm draped around a friend, I somehow got on the plane. I couldn't stand up straight; I could only hunch over, but the thought of being left behind alone was too awful for words. Peter [Martins] told the officials that when we arrived at Copenhagen, I was to have a wheelchair and an ambulance. They refused. They said they didn't want any bad publicity; they wanted everything to look just perfect. Peter pitched a fit. They acted like the KGB.

"When we got to Denmark, they led me down the steps as though nothing were wrong. I started to faint; they didn't care. They walked me over to a little Volkswagen and shoved me in, smacking my head on the door as they pushed. The drove me to the ambulance, which was parked out of sight; then they wouldn't take out the stretcher. I had to struggle out of the VW and crawl into the ambulance. I stayed for a week. I wanted to go on and meet everyone in Paris, but I just couldn't. I came home for treatment. I went to the chiropractor, scared to death. Then I called my sister and said, 'Meet me at Caramba.' Between the treatments and the margaritas, I realized I would live. I have never felt pain like that in my whole life. Still, I always knew my back would get better. When my knee was so bad, I was one step away from knocking on the ballet mistress's door to tell her I was through."

Another chapter in Lavery's life began in the spring of 1984. At that time brand-new pressures conspired to give him a more subtle physical problem, an ulcer. Peter Martins had just retired from dancing in order to take over for Mr. Balanchine, and Lavery and Ib Andersen were learning all the repertory that once had been the domain of their new boss. Talk about competition! Louis XIV would have loved it. What tension! One can assume it was not a bit easier for the prematurely retired Martins to let go of his star vehicles than it was for Lavery to have missed premiering *Ballade*.

One can also assume that joy and doubt and fear and ambition were all jumbled up every day in the studio where the three men worked. One can also assume that it was somewhat harder for Martins to teach his roles to Lavery than it was for him to pass them on to Andersen. Though Martins and Ib are countrymen, the younger Dane is slight and dark; physically he resembles the older not at all. Lavery is tall, blond, princely, big . . . as is Martins. Andersen was adding new parts to his repertoire; Lavery was stepping into Martins's shoes. The public even expected that Sean would take over for Peter. (There were some who couldn't tell the two apart. One devoted fan wrote a torrid love letter to Sean Martins. The two men opened the missive together, had a good chuckle over it together, and threw it out *à deux* as well.) Those months in the early spring of 1984 were tough for all concerned, but Lavery kept swallowing and smiling until he got an ulcer. "I needed to feel Peter's approval," he says. "And he was just unable to open up with me. It was awful. I thought I was going to have to strap on a chin or something," he says, laughingly referring to the Dane's jutting jaw. "Finally I just went to him and said, 'You have to help me.' He did. I think maybe I might have enjoyed that time if I were more of a shark, but I'm just not.

"I used to take *soooooo* much cr*aaa*p," continues Lavery. "That's why I got the ulcer. I was trying to please everybody, as usual. I was just holding everything in and being too nice. Later Peter told me I had to learn to scream more. I have learned now, and it always works. People are so surprised when I scream at them. They don't expect it from me.

"Coping with everything has been the hardest part of being a dancer for me," he says. "The training and the work have always gone just fine, but all the other stuff and all the games people can play. . . . We start so young . . . and we really are so adult in our discipline, so focused . . . but because we're dancers, we can vege out in other ways. We are like disciplined little children, and we are treated like children long after we've become adults. It's hard for dancers to grow up. Sometimes in class a teacher will say, 'Hold your tummy in now.' I want to say "G*iiiiivvvveee* me a b*rrr-reeeeeaaaaak.* I'm pushin' thirty, Mama.' Then I realize that it's not their fault, that that's the way they were brought up too. So I just say, 'I beg your pardon? Oh, you want me to hold my stomach in? Okay, fine.' I feel like I have a grip on it all now, like I'm going to be a normal humanoid. It's a game for me to see if I can make it through a whole season without missing a single performance. And I can do it. Jacques d'Amboise told me that this was the time that I should enjoy, that these next years would be the best . . . all the struggling to get here is in the past, and the hurting too much to go on is in the future. I try to remember that and try to keep my sense of humor. I'm a big believer in laughing."

Max laughed all the time, too, until hip surgery at age fifteen permanently altered his attitude about playing hurt. Before the operation he could and would do anything; he was utterly carefree about his body, confident of his immortality, impervious to cautionary tales. His first New York winter, during his first snow and his first *Nutcracker,* Max slipped on the ice one day during a snowball war, crashed in a heap, and broke a bone in his wrist. It hurt like hell but it never stopped him for a moment, even though he had to have a cast. He took class in his cast, he ran around with it on, and he even performed in *Nuts* with his plaster casing hidden beneath his party-goer's ruffled sleeve.

After his operation everything was different. Max tried to forget about what it was like—the pain, the crutches, the weakness. He wanted to forget about it, to resume his devil-may-care fearlessness, and he pretended to himself and everyone else that he was indeed the same old Mad Max, that nothing had changed. But even success in San Francisco couldn't cure what ailed him. Max couldn't trust his body anymore; he didn't know what would happen. He was vulnerable, mortal, destructible. He had lost his confidence; he had become timid and afraid of injury. Risk was no longer something that appealed to him, at least not in dance class, and now a fourth year in Intermediate, another year of staring daily into that same mirror, that same hostile piece of glass, didn't help the situation any, either. Max joined the sad list of damaged dance students, and he began giving in to every ache and pain that came his way, always afraid that something drastic was happening. For weeks he stopped classes after the barre exercises because his back hurt. Finally he got himself to a physical therapist who manipulated away the muscle spasm and his fears.

One day he wouldn't finish class because "there's something wrong with my knee. I get it from cabrioles or big jumps when I come down on my left foot." Another day it would be: "My shoes are so tight. I don't know what's wrong. I must have bruised my feet or something." Once he stopped right in the middle of partnering class, his favorite, because "I have a pain on the right side of my neck from having girls sit on my shoulder." The litany grew and grew, even including worry about his heart, concern that it was not beating properly. Anxiety became his middle name, and he got excused from class or took only the first part, the barre, all the time. Krammie called him "Lezzy boy," and Ms. Finn, who took attendance, regularly said, "Always some excuse, Max."

Once he even called in to say he wouldn't be there because he had to go buy a jacket to wear to a City Ballet gala performance the next day. Charlie had given him tickets, and he was taking an adorable bunhead, but he had no appropriate clothes. He talked his mother into getting him a sport jacket, but she insisted on taking him shopping at a time when he should have been dancing. The next day he left class early to get dressed for the fancy fund-raising event. Mrs. Gleboff had been surprised and disapproving that sartorial splendor was taking priority over Mr. Rapp, but she was sweet with Max, insisting that he show her how he looked in his new tweeds and murmuring her approval of his choice of tie.

Says Richard Rapp, "It's hard to figure Max. He has some ability, but he's been handicapped by injuries. It looks like he doesn't care; he gets frustrated and disgusted. But I don't know. Ballet is so physically demanding, especially on bodies that are developing. You can't put forth the effort that is necessary when you are injured all the time."

Says Max, "If I were a girl, I would definitely not still be dancing."

XV.

Despair

Not long after Max finished his *Nutcracker* stint with Mid-Atlantic, his mother found the apartment of her dreams, a co-op sublet with an option to buy, three blocks from SAB. Brenda had always wanted to be nearer to the school than they were, closer to the action. Now she hoped her son would be around home more and would bring his dancing friends with him. Their new apartment was a better place to bring people home to, in Brenda's opinion; it was more like a home. (Max had told his mother he was ashamed to bring kids home to their old apartment, that it was too crummy. He really didn't care; he didn't want to bring his friends home because they couldn't smoke or talk freely, but "I certainly wasn't going to tell her that," says Max.)

Their new building is an old one, with some old-world charm and elegance. It's huge, U-shaped, with two entrances and a central courtyard. Theirs is the western tower; their apartment is on the tenth floor. Once again Max was granted the best room, his sister the lesser. Once again their mother didn't get a room of her own at all. This time the living room has become Brenda's living, sleeping, and working quarters—also where they eat, watch television, and entertain, when they entertain. Brenda doesn't mind, though. She loves the place, loves its fireplace and walnut woodwork, its romance and its history. The building was built for artists; to this day dancers, writers, actors, and painters inhabit many of the apartments. Now the Fuquas live there too. Brenda doesn't even mind that her kitchen has a moving-about width of exactly eighteen inches. Gourmet cooking is not anywhere on her agenda. "I could be happy here for the rest of my life," she says. "I just hope I can somehow come up with enough money to buy it."

The new apartment is also close to PCS, and Brenda agreed at last to send Max there for the spring semester. She had the money now, and something had to be done about the boy's schooling. So, even if it meant he would be only with kids who performed or wanted to perform, she decided PCS was okay, and besides, anything would be better than his not doing his correspondence courses. Another term had flown by without Max's sending in any completed work.

He was now a year and a half behind. At the end of the summer Brenda had gone to their minister to seek help in finding a proctor for Max, someone to see that the boy did his lessons and mailed them in, someone to supervise the required exams. She didn't know where else to look but church, and she hadn't been able to afford a tutor. Brenda thought that it would be a good idea to have a man do the job, that a strong male presence would be very good for Max, that he could use a non-dancing adult male role model and example-setter. The minister agreed with her and said he would give the matter some consideration. Soon he announced that he had just the guy, a church member, a smart and strong man who, he thought, would be happy to take on the task as a volunteer, as a good deed. Brenda and Max met the volunteer and they both liked him. He was big and fun and full of energy. An arrangement was made. The example-setter and role model had to cancel their first appointment, however, because he had an urgent prior commitment with his parole board. It seems he had just been released from the pokey, where he had spent a little time for a little white-collar crime. No wonder good deeds were so high on the list of the strong male presence. PCS looked better and better all the time, but there was no tuition money until after the Eighty-ninth Street apartment had been sold.

Finally it was; Max and his mother and sister moved into their new home, and Max applied to PCS. He was accepted into the tenth grade and started classes in February, as a soon-to-be-seventeen-year-old sophomore. He hated being so far behind, was embarrassed being in with "the little teenyboppers," but basically liked the kids and enjoyed his classes. One or two of his teachers he really liked. He was also glad to be back on some sort of forward track, even if it did mean giving up his freedom, his job as one of Charlie's messengers, and his salary of fifty dollars a week. Max had saved a little money from his *Nutcracker*-ing, and Leslie Otto had hired him again for her spring program. Once again he ventured out to Westchester every weekend to rehearse with the Mid-Atlantic Ballet. Ben was not there this time—he was after far bigger fish—but Bryant was, and so were several Ottos. Max was out in Westchester the Sunday Joe Duell committed suicide. Leslie had heard something awful had happened; Max called Charlie for the details.

Joe and his older brother, Dan, were NYCB principals from Dayton, Ohio. They started dance lessons when the Dayton Ballet promised scholarships to any males who could pass an audition. The boys' father had been unable to resist.

He had always wanted to dance but had been forbidden to do so by his own father, a strict Methodist minister. Now was his chance; he and his two sons, aged seven and ten and a half at the time, auditioned together, got scholarships together, and took class together. After a year or two Duell père dropped out, but the boys kept on. That was in the mid-sixties; SAB staffers had Ford Foundation money to spend and were out and about, looking for new talent. Dan was spotted and brought to New York; Joe followed after a time. Nature hadn't designed Joe's body with classical dance in mind; neither had she blessed him with copious quantities of natural facility. The muses, though, had given his soul a passion for ballet that made him insist on becoming the best danseur he possibly could, the best choreographer, and the best teacher. He planned to do all three; his life would be spent in dance. It was. Joe said he knew instantly, at age seven, that he would choreograph, and he later vowed that when he stopped dancing and started teaching, he would teach young men to do much more than jump and turn, he would insist that they learn all the gestures that added up to poetry.

Being Dan's younger brother was hard for Joe, even though he claimed, "There was never overt competition between us." Comparisons were unavoidable, though, and for years the older brother was far ahead of the younger. Joe didn't think he would ever be as good a dancer as Dan; he didn't think he'd ever be much of a dancer, period. "My bad feelings were always that I thought I should be doing better," he said almost two years before his death. Five years before that, Joe's bad feelings forced him to leave ballet for a time, to get a respite from the pressures he felt so intensely, to be treated for the depression that would haunt him throughout the rest of his brief life. Physically Joe was strong; emotionally he was fragile. He was an intelligent man, articulate, a musician and a ballet scholar. He'd gone through high school so fast, in spite of his dance studies, that he'd had a year of college before he even came to SAB at age eighteen. College was of little use to Joe, however. He was bewitched by ballet, totally devoted to dance.

And on a drab Sunday morning in February, at the age of twenty-nine, Joe Duell was dead, having jumped from his apartment window and been found by a neighbor on the pavement below. Lincoln Kirstein always called him the Continuity. Now the succession was brutally broken.

Most ballet companies regard themselves as a family, and the New York City Ballet is no exception. Joe's brothers and sisters in spirit were as shocked and shaken as his blood kin at the taking of his own life. It was such a violent act; it spoke of such desperation and despair. Joe had been anything but violent, and apparently no one among them had realized the full extent of his despair. Many of his colleagues found out about his death on arrival at the theater for the Sunday matinee. He had been scheduled to dance; an announcement was made, and many tears were shed. But the performance was held, weak knees and all, in Joe's honor.

Joe's passing marked the third time death had come to the City Ballet family in its very recent history. First Mr. Balanchine went, leaving everyone feeling like abandoned children. Then John Bass died amid speculation about whether he did or did not suffer from AIDS, and a different kind of anxiety spread through the family. And now Joe was gone. Why? What had happened? The other two, at least, had been sick, physically and noticeably ill. Everyone felt inadequate and helpless. They all knew that Joe had a history of depression, that he had been treated for it for years. Of late they all had seen him looking pained and disheveled as well. But no one had thought it would end like this. Most of Joe's colleagues had fought bouts of doubt and fear or depression themselves, and they all had come through them eventually. So, as in so many families, no one really had understood what was going on with Joe, and no one had known how to help him.

Those who knew him, those who had seen him dance, and those who had just read about his suicide in the newspapers were saddened at the death of the handsome dancer with what seemed like such a bright future. The speculation this time centered on a female psychic he and several other dancers in the company had been consulting. How had she influenced Joe? Had she somehow tipped the balance for him? Sides were chosen, camps established, and enmities cemented. In their terror and confusion Joe's friends tried to figure out who or what to blame for taking him from them. Finally it wouldn't matter. Nothing would bring him back.

On Monday Max went to the funeral service in a Catholic church not far from the theater. He heard Joe's father talk about his younger son; he heard Joe's brother, Dan, play the flute and their sister read something she had written about her dead brother. Then it was over. Max didn't go to class that day or the next. "I just couldn't," he says. "I was too depressed. It wasn't as though I'd known him real well or anything, but we would talk sometimes in the dressing room. All I could do those two days was lie around. It was awful."

Within a month Max's sister, Alice, was dead too. She was twenty-three. Max and his mother and sister Brenda flew to Albuquerque to get Alice's body and take it to Louisiana to be buried in a family plot. When they came back to New York, Max tried to pretend that he was just fine, that things were normal, but he was pale and thin, wan-looking. He seemed more vulnerable somehow, weaker. His eyes were expressionless, and his voice was softer, less lively, older. Max's mother tried to keep up a brave, cheerful front as well, but it kept catching up with her. For days at a time she was unable to leave their apartment; she couldn't even go to the grocery store. Later Brenda would claim that she really wasn't so sad that Alice was gone, that "God has a plan for exactly how many days all of us spend on earth, and we wouldn't want to try to change his plan, would we?" Her pain was very evident, though, her protestations hollow, her broken heart in plain view on the sleeve of her mourning-black dress.

There were several versions of how Alice died. Charlie said he had been told that she fell off a chair or down a flight of stairs; he wasn't sure which. Max said his sister had inherited a blood disease from her father's side of the family (not his) and that she fainted regularly; that this time, when she fainted, she hit her head. Max felt that Alice was "better off dead," that "It may sound weird . . .," but she had been so unhappy, so unable to deal with living, that being "in God's hands" was the best solution for her, that God would take care of her now. Brenda Fuqua said that they weren't entirely sure what had killed Alice; that she had fallen in her bathroom and broken her neck but that she had also been in a motorbike accident a week or so before her death and that perhaps a blood clot had gone to her brain and actually killed her, and that when she fell and broke her neck, maybe she was already dead. Brenda said that an autopsy to find out the cause had not been scheduled. The Albuquerque medical examiner's office says Alice died of "acute and chronic alcoholism."

Joe Duell committed suicide the fast way, crashing to an end on the concrete sidewalk outside his apartment. Alice

Mullen did herself in the slow way, ounce by ounce, sip by sip. Both took portions of their survivors with them, bits of the hearts of all who were close to them, who would never again be able to feel the same joy and elation they had felt before Joe and Alice died, who would always wonder what they missed, what they might have done differently.

XVI.

Growing Up

And then it was the middle of March again, just past the ides. The sun began slanting through the studio windows from a loftier angle than it had just days before, and it offered stronger solace to the taut, winter-weary muscles inside. When the SAB boys took off for Central Park now, they left their mufflers behind, and they waded through masses of purple and yellow crocuses on the park's paths, softballs in their hands, in preparation for spring's official arrival. Almost a whole year had elapsed since Max pasted Josh one in class. The two continued to ignore each other, but both were calmer, more subdued, maybe a little resigned. They were also growing up.

Josh had been in Advanced Men's since fall, and it was his turn now to be the one taking academics by correspondence—only he was actually doing his. In another reversal, his ballet life had gone to hell: His early promise was rapidly vanishing, literally being stretched too thin. Josh was growing so fast, he was like the rose in one of those stop-action films, unfolding before his own eyes, from bud to bloom: 6'2" and still climbing. In seven months he had added four vertical inches to his teenage frame. He could hardly find the ends of his fingers now, much less feel as though he had any control at all over his body. Every day he found his strength siphoned off a little more, and every week there were additions to the list of ballet moves he was once able to do well and now could hardly execute. Stanley's class was a surreal nightmare for him, Krammie's just a bad dream. "I can hardly wait to see what they say in my evaluation," he commented with a sardonic chuckle.

Evaluations are one of the two annual rites of passage that preoccupy SAB students each spring; the other is Workshop. Workshop is for the graduating students; evaluations are for all. Each year each dancer is evaluated. For weeks before, Mrs. Gleboff appears in every class, notebook in hand. She sits down next to the teacher, and the two confer, first talking about one dancer, then another, while she makes careful notes of what is being seen and what is being said. At the first sight of the school's director, the dynamic in the room changes. No one is quite sure what is being looked at, or whom, so everyone assumes it is he, and everyone tries extra hard to be the very best in the group. They all also try to eavesdrop or read lips, but teacher and director are too smart—and too discreet—for them. Says one young danseur, "It's so nerve-racking; it's like an audition." He's partially right. It isn't quite *like* an audition, however; it *is* an audition, an unannounced audition. This is when each student's situation is assessed; the school will now decide what his next step should be and whether they think he is on the road to becoming a Poet of Gesture. Every student at SAB has more than one teacher, and Mrs. Gleboff consults with all of them about every student. Progress is calculated, in dancing and in body development; attitude and ability are judged. Talent is not a word that is used at SAB; ability takes its place. Talent is too amorphous; it hints at promise. Ability is clear, concrete. One can see ability; one can decide just how able a student dancer is. Each teacher tells Mrs. Gleboff what he or she thinks the student's strong points are, as well as what he needs to concentrate on the most.

Then, in June, students are called into the director's office one at a time to hear their fates. It's more intense than an interview; it's more like having to sit quietly and listen to a detailed accounting of your final exams, subject by subject. In their evaluations students learn the truth according to their teachers, and they also learn whether they will be advancing to the next level or staying where they are, or whether they should start thinking about taking college board exams in the fall. Mrs. Gleboff is gentle, if impassive, and as kind as possible. She always stresses that she is just the deliverer of the tidings either glad or sad, not the originator, and that the teachers are the ones who make the judgments.

For the kids who are destined to be the principals of tomorrow, evaluations are great. The sessions give them a chance to bask in sung praises and to have their promotions officially announced. The top kids come out of their evaluations beaming, walking a little taller, feeling a little surer about their futures. For them, the meetings offer reward for hard work done well. For others, they offer rejection and humiliation; for some, they are torture. Evaluations can mean having to confront unwanted truths and sometimes ending long-dreamed-of-dreams. A poor evaluation can also mean trouble at home. Obsessed ballet mothers or fathers don't want to hear bad news any more than obsessed dancers do, and those who live through their children's accomplishments can be very threatened by setbacks or lack of approval. So, in addition to talking to every student every year, Mrs. Gleboff has to deal with disappointed, outraged, or challenging parents, too, those who cannot or will not accept the verdict that has been handed down. Meanwhile the child in question has to deal with being insufficient, embarrassed, inferior to his classmates, and caught betwen the two adult camps. It can be excruciating.

Workshop is the SAB ritual for seniors; it's the culmination of their time spent at SAB. Every May, a weekend full of performances is scheduled to represent graduation, prom night, and first professional audition all wrapped into one—Workshop. There are no valedictory addresses delivered for SAB students; no awards for scholarship are presented. Instead, parts in Workshop are granted. A solo in a new work choreographed on the student by boss Peter Martins equals summa cum laude. A solo in a new work choreographed for the student by someone other than Peter Martins: magna. Leads in already existing ballets are the equivalent of cum laude. Corps members make up the remainder of the graduates.

Audiences for Workshop performances are special; they consist of a smattering of dance lovers and regular ballet-goers, a large population of other dancers coming in to check out the latest competition, scores of adoring parents and grandparents, and many directors of ballet companies here and abroad. Monday, the last night, is party night. Each year the Juilliard theater fills with Big Spenders, the patrons who support SAB and who dress up, check each other out as assiduously as they view the dancers on the stage, and adjourn to the third-floor studios after the show for an elegant little supper. Saturday night, the Junior Committee is in full view, the Philistines of Tomorrow. They are designer-clad and tied in black just as their parents will be on Monday, and they view this all-important (to the students) night as another event on a crowded social calendar, a plum event to be sure but still just one of many.

The press is here too; Workshop performances and performers get reviewed in all the newspapers and dance magazines. The most important viewers of this spectacle, though, are those influential folks who have total power of balletic life or death over the student dancers, the company directors. Ballet companies from coast to coast (and in Europe too) are now run by believers in Balanchine. So the SAB ethic and style are more widely welcome and understood now than ever before. The boys still have it all over the girls, though. There are many more lovely and capable ballerinas than there are jobs for lovely and capable ballerinas, but any male dancer who makes it through to Advanced Men's at SAB is virtually guaranteed employment—somewhere.

SAB students want more than anything to join the New York City Ballet, just as Hotchkiss kids want to go to Yale and Lawrenceville students to Princeton. You don't go to a top preparatory school to get into your local community college. Likewise with dance. Some at SAB are so intent that they say they wouldn't dream of dancing anywhere else, that it's NYCB or nothing. Others include ABT on their list; if they don't get jobs with one or the other, they say, they will forget the whole thing. Still others say, "I love to dance, I want to dance, and I have to dance. I've spent years and years studying dance. Most of all I'd like to get into City or ABT or another top company, but if I can't, I'll dance wherever I have to. If I have to go to East Overshoe, I will, and happily."

Scattered throughout the patrons and Junior Committee members and balletomanes and proud mothers at Workshop are the men with the contracts, looking to see just who is who and what gaps in their ranks they can fill with freshly minted SAB dancers. It is just as exciting for a company director to spot and land a new talent as it is for that talent to be spotted and landed. Directors and choreographers need new bodies and fresh approaches; dancers are their material and their inspiration. Out front the talk is all of "Don't miss so-and-so; her extension is amazing" and "What's-his-name is a terrific partner; keep your eye on him." Backstage, the rumor mill churns away. "When is Misha due? Is Helgi here from San Francisco? Is that Ricky Weiss with Peter? Who's with Mrs. Bass? Has Villella filled all the spots in Miami? Who's here from Europe?" Buzz, buzz, buzz, buzz. By performance time everyone knows—or thinks he knows—just who is there from what company and where he is sitting. The excitement and anticipation help the dancers psych themselves to go out there and bring the audience figuratively to its knees and then literally to its feet for a standing ovation.

Generally Workshop solos are danced by different dancers for each performance, to spread around opportunities. That means each has but one chance to wow whoever is there. Every move, every tiny step, becomes the most important move or tiny step in the world, in the whole history of ballet. Sometimes the pressure builds too high. One year a very promising young ballerina cracked under it; in her fear she lost her footing and fell. Nothing could assuage her sobs after the mishap; little could make her feel better about herself; no one could convince her it was not the end of the world. Right then and there she gave up ballet entirely.

Workshop casts are chosen long in advance of the performance dates, so they can rehearse and rehearse and rehearse. The dancers are in the studio for as long as four months before anyone puts so much as a single digit on the stage. Being in Workshop therefore takes on an even greater meaning to students than graduation, prom, and audition. From late winter until May, everyone's concentration is on Workshop. Once again to be chosen becomes all; the caste system is firmly in place. "No, I can't do this today; I have rehearsal for Workshop. No, I can't do that tomorrow either; I have rehearsal for Workshop." Rank and status are clearly defined by participation in Workshop; to be left out is to suffer banishment.

Neither Max nor Josh had parts in Workshop. Commented Max with a shrug, "It's not the same as it used to be. Workshop doesn't mean as much as it always did." Says City Ballet principal and SAB graduate Jock Soto, "If you don't have a lead in Workshop, you're nothing."

He ought to know. Soto had a lead in 1981, in Peter Martins's new ballet *The Magic Flute*. From Workshop, Soto danced right into the company and right on up the ladder to principal dancer. At age twenty. Michael Byars ought to know too. Soto's Workshop lead had once been his. It was Byars with whom Martins worked when he was first making the new ballet. Then, one day, the rehearsal schedule was posted, and Soto was in and Byars out. That's how Michael found out he had been replaced; that's how dancers often find out they've been replaced; no reason given, and they daren't ask for one. Byars had parts in other ballets that year, but still he was crushed, and he went through Workshop feeling that indeed he was nothing, nothing at all.

The next year Byars had his Workshop lead, and the following fall Martins glided over to him one day after class and told him he'd been made a City Ballet apprentice; that meant he would continue at SAB, but he could also take

Workshop
rehearsals go on
for months.

215

company class and appear in three ballets over the year. This momentous news he learned in the hallway, on his way to the dressing room after class. Just like that; not even one trumpet. "It was like my birthday," says Byars. "If that hadn't happened, I would have had a very different attitude. . . ." Then in May, Michael got a contract with the City Ballet, and he became a full-fledged member of the staff.

If graduating into the company is a dream come true, it is also the most drastic transition a danseur makes during his career: from student to pro in one not-so-easy leap. Suddenly all protective wraps are gone; the dancer is naked and alone. There is no safety net, no sheltered classroom, no gentle nurturer like Stanley. The company is the big time, and the danseur must change from aspirant who gets four months to rehearse one ballet for four performances to trooper who is on every night, sometimes in a ballet he has learned only that morning. When Soto was first in the pros, he had such severe stage fright that he regularly vomited before making an entrance. He was just sixteen years old.

Byars was nineteen when he gained admittance. He had graduated from Stuyvesant High, been a presidential scholar, and he had even gone to college. Still, the adjustment was huge. Says he, "Workshop really isn't enough to prepare you. Your view of yourself and your view of the dancing world really changes when you get into the company. At SAB, if you're among the best, if you're first in Workshop, you think you're the best in the whole world. And at the school you take one, maybe two, classes a day; you work on a limited number of things. Then you're in the company. Every day you have class, then five hours of rehearsal, then a costume fitting, and then you dance in three different ballets at night. There's never enough time. Sometimes I do five ballets in one day—

matinee and evening. There's no time to prepare for each
different ballet; you just get out there and do them."

He continues, "In the company you learn you are not
the only one, that yours is not the only style. You start to work
with the director and the ballet master. Having a boss really
affects your attitude. Peter can be mean, and he's been mean
to me. Jerry Robbins has been mean to me too. But you can't
always be satisfied with what the director thinks. You have to
think for yourself; you have to believe in yourself. That's
another big difference. In the company you have to be
everything to yourself—teacher, coach, everything—and
then get out onstage. I feel like I'm on my own so much now
that I'm interested in any opinion, whether I agree or think
it's crazy."

Since joining City Ballet, Michael has had a chance to
dance several soloist parts as well as his corps roles, and he has
had a ballet, *Eight More*, made on him by the Boss. Martins
used three young men for the ballet; it's a funny, lighthearted, frolicking work that audiences love. It's also extremely difficult; it demands speedy, tricky virtuosity from all
three dancers. And every time out, it leaves them ex-
hausted—empty and full at the same time. Says Byars, "It
takes me several hours to come down from *Eight More*. When
my family came to see it for the first time, I was hoping they
would give me corrections afterward, but they were too
excited themselves."

Michael is very close to his family. "I couldn't do it
without them," he says. He grew up around the State Theater—his father is an oboist with the NYCB orchestra.
Michael wanted to dance from a very early age, but he was
afraid to ask his father if he could start lessons. "It just didn't
seem normal to me, wanting to dance," he recalls. He never

Left to right,
Peter Boal,
Gen Horiyuchi,
and Michael Byars
in *Eight More*.

© Paul Kolnik

did have to gather up his courage and confront his father, though; George Balanchine interceded for him. One day Mr. B. suggested to Michael's dad that he bring the boy over to SAB. Mr. Byars was delighted. "It's really weird around the company," says Michael now. "Mr. Balanchine's name is never mentioned. It's like a superstition. I never had a chance to work with him. He never had a direct influence on me— except, of course, for my being a dancer in the first place," he adds with a giggle.

Unlike Soto and so many others, Michael has never had a problem with stage fright. He loves to dance in front of an audience. "If you're a dancer, you have to be seen," he says. "That's what it's all about. Performing is the most fun of all. You go through so much to do it, and then it's like opening the gates. It makes everything worthwhile. It's now the reason I work."

XVII.

Evaluations

After Max's second appearance with the Mid-Atlantic Ballet, his only opportunities to be out onstage came when he filled in as the City Ballet flower boy. The flower boy is the person who brings out the bouquets and presents them to the ballerina as she takes her bows. On special occasions, like a debut in a role, or opening night, or closing night, or a first appearance after a long time of injury, or merely if she has a particularly ardent admirer, a ballerina receives bouquets. Mothers and husbands and suitors say it with flowers. Always Lincoln Kirstein does, too, so sometimes several bunches arrive at a time. The flower boy presents all the cards to each dancer before her performance. Sometimes she elects to receive all her tribute onstage; other times only the most important blossoms are selected as the ones to be publicly presented. The flower boy then slips into a tuxedo provided by management, combs his hair, and watches the show from backstage, waiting to do his work. He gets paid five dollars per performance, but the real incentive is the chance to view the proceedings from the wings, to feel like a member of the group. Brandon was the regular flower boy, John the most frequent substitute; but once in a while they were both busy, and Max got to fill in.

Unlike Josh, Max hadn't changed much over the year from March to March. He had grown only about an inch, so he hadn't lost any strength or balance, but he hadn't gained a whole lot, either. He had missed too many classes, stopped partway through too many times, refused to take Mr. Rapp's instructions to heart too often. Every day he heard the same corrections; every day he decided they were unnecessary, that he was doing things the right way. Finally Mr. Rapp got so frustrated by Max's resistance that he took the boy aside and told him, "You're a fool not to listen to me, Max. You're never going to get anywhere if you don't do it my way."

Says Max, "In some ways I believe what everyone says. In other ways . . . oh, I don't know. Mostly I think, 'I'm only sixteen, I don't want to deal with this.' It puts a lot of restrictions on you."

Every day Max appeared at PCS—usually late, semi-prepared, and reeking of smoke—but he was there. His classes started at nine A.M. and ended shortly after two in the afternoon. Ballet class wasn't until five-thirty, and most of Max's pals were too busy with Workshop rehearsals to go off on pizza forays with him these afternoons. The Juilliard lounge was sparsely populated this time of the year, too, so Max often whiled away the time in between schools by himself. Sometimes he went home; other times he hung out in coffee shops or the pizza parlor. One day he was passing some minutes in a local hamburger joint, chewing on an all-American infusion of grease, when he was joined by City Ballet dancer Peter Naumann.

Naumann is a senior corps member with the NYCB;

he was also the thirteen-year-old Bluebird in that Carlisle, Pennsylvania, production of *Sleeping Beauty* that turned Sean Lavery on to the joys of dance. Naumann was hard-pressed to list any joys for himself on that blustery afternoon. He was thirty-one years old, he'd been dancing for more than twenty years, his knees were killing him, and he was pooped. "*Maaa*n," says Max, "he was so bummed out. All he could talk about was how he wanted to retire, but he didn't know what to do, that he'd blown off school, that he'd only danced his whole life, that his wife was a dancer, too, and that he didn't know how he could possibly make a living any other way, much less support a family. It was terrifying. I finally said to him, 'Hey, man, I'm only sixteen years old!' Then I practically ran out of there."

By April, Max decided he'd better buckle down. He was feeling a little less achy and painy, things were okay at PCS, and evaluations loomed. He knew his had to be a good one, that he had to get promoted to Advanced or he would be asked to leave. "The worst would be if they told me I had to stay in Intermediate," he said, shocked at the sudden thought. "Oh, they couldn't! They wouldn't! If they did, I'd have to quit. I wouldn't be able to stand it. Can you imagine it? Five years in Intermediate?!"

So, just as he always crammed for exams, Max started cramming for his evaluation. Every day he came to class properly dressed. Sometimes he even remembered to remove his watch. Every day he worked harder than he had in months, and almost every day he stayed for the full class. He stopped squinting at himself in the mirror, and he paid attention to what the teacher said. One day his mother watched her son's class; parents are permitted to look on once in a while. Afterward Brenda Fuqua extolled, "I was really impressed. This was not that boy who looked so lazy last year. This was someone else, a really lovely dancer. He's come a very long way." Max beamed a megakilowatt smile. The praise was coming from the person who meant more to him than Mr. Rapp and Krammie and Stanley put together, the person who meant the most to him in the whole world, the one whose opinion really counted, to whom he went for counsel and for comfort, and whom he described as his best friend. Clearly he believed her.

Max wasn't the only person putting on a little added effort at SAB. Everyone seemed extra-energized; all the classes were more supercharged than usual. For some it had to do with Workshop; others, like Max, wanted a better evaluation than they thought they were entitled to. It was more than that, though. By spring, young bodies really start to respond to all the hours of toil they have been undergoing since September. Says Stanley Williams, "Something always starts to happen around this time of year. You can't push; you have to be very patient. They hear it when they're ready to hear it. Suddenly someone surprises you. Suddenly that boy starts to pick it up."

No teachers want their students to succeed any more than SAB teachers do. So when someone like Max starts to show a little more interest and availability to instruction, the teacher homes in and tries to capitalize on the newfound enthusiasm. As soon as Max started paying more attention to him, Richard Rapp started paying more attention to Max. Says Rapp, "When I first started teaching, I was so impatient. It took me a long time to accept the fact that I am not going to get quick results. Now I've got more patience; now I'm more realistic. What makes all this worthwhile is when you see a good dancer onstage and can say, 'Hey, I had a hand in that.' That's the big reward."

Among his recommendations for Max, Mr. Rapp said he thought the boy should be promoted to Advanced. He saw no reason to keep him back any longer, and maybe a vote of confidence would be what he really needed to surge ahead. Besides, Rapp felt he'd basically done all he could with Max; it was now up to the boy to decide whether he would go forward or not. Stanley thought Max should come to his class too. Stanley is a confirmed optimist; he is always eager to give a student a try. Once he even kept in school a rebellious young Dane who would later become his boss. Officials at the Royal Danish school wanted to throw out the teenage Peter Martins for his mutinous behavior, for skipping class and violating the dress code, for lack of respect. Stanley thought it would be a terrible waste, that what you should do with a gifted and defiant youth is teach and mold him, not expel and reject him. He said that if Peter went, he would go too. Luckily the officials in Copenhagen relented. If both Williams and Martins had ended up working for Georg Jensen rather than George Balanchine, the state of the male dancer would be a very sorry one indeed.

Workshop weekend was full of excitement. The performances were all sold out, and the audiences resonated with talk about how exceptionally good the boys were. Even Charlie, who usually refused to admit that the boys even existed, was found extolling the virtues of this particular crop. Ben from Belgium was the star of the weekend. He danced like an experienced pro in a new Peter Martins pas de deux which had been made on him just days before. He was elegant, skillful, and regal. Two of the American boys—Jerry and Gordon—showed that they were ready to exit the cocoon and seek fame and fortune. Rob, the big blond puppy Rob, convinced everyone that he would be a serious force in a year or so. Nilas was excellent and even handsomer than his father.

The corps boys got invaluable performing experience and started envisioning themselves in the leads next year. Misha did show up, as did directors from several other companies, and Max's friend Peter even got a job offer from San Francisco, an event both joyous and perplexing at the same time. It was like getting early acceptance at Penn when your first choice is Harvard. He didn't know what to do. Should he accept the offer and give up hopes of joining City? Or should he say no and stay at SAB another year? Would he lose out on a job altogether? Would his chances of getting into NYCB be any better if he stayed? There was only one way to find out, so he mustered all the courage he could find, and then some, and made an appointment to talk with the Boss. Martins could only hint at future opportunities; he could offer no guarantees. But the intimations were strong enough to convince the younger Peter to stay on the East Coast for another year.

On the Saturday night of the Workshop, Max went over to the Juilliard theater early to wish his chums well and to get in on a little of the pre-performance excitement. He didn't stay to see the dancing, though; he had to get over to the State Theater and be flower boy for the City Ballet. Josh did the flowers for the Workshop performers; the two shared more than either would ever know.

The day after Workshop everyone was back in class as usual, but there was no feeling of letdown. Triumph filled the air, and how great everyone had been became the main subject of conversation. The students who hadn't participated now were able to share in the reflected glory of those who had done so well; they were all united by success. Even the teachers and administrators fussed a little over their new luminaries, and congratulations were accepted with assured grace.

June drew near, and Max could hardly wait. He wanted the year to end, and he wanted to find out that he'd been promoted to Advanced. He knew he would be, and he already knew how he was going to spend his summer. He had been invited to Heather Watts's school in Saratoga. His mother didn't want him to go; she thought he should get a job and earn a little money, but he knew he could get around her once he had his promotion in hand. And it was only for July. He could work all of August. Max had turned seventeen, it was now or never. He looked forward so much to saying goodbye to Intermediate and to taking his place at Stanley's barre. He could practically taste it. And what would he do if he weren't sent ahead? "Cry for a month," he said.

All at once three of Max's friends gave up dancing altogether. First Mark, the talented redhead. Mark had grown up elegantly. He was tall, graceful, and broad-shouldered; he even walked beautifully; every day he looked more and more like a freckled-face *danseur noble* and less and less like Howdy Doody. And suddenly he quit. Max couldn't understand why. Mark had everything going for him; he was sure to be hired by ABT. Mark could only say that he was tired of ballet, that he wanted a more "normal" life. Maybe that was true, but his young mother had recently dropped dead of a heart attack, and it seems safe to assume that this terrible shock played a big part in his decision.

Then Andrew called it a day, finally deciding to give up battling his bruised body and concentrate on molding his mind. Now his problem was where he should go to college. Margaret was already in the City Ballet, so Drew wanted to study in New York and be near his ladylove. On the other hand, his professor-father could get him free tuition at an upstate college. It was a dilemma, but it didn't matter to Max. He knew that wherever Drew went, he would be lost to him

1986 was a banner
year for talented
boys at SAB.

now. Damn that Margaret. Ilan left SAB too—to pay full attention to his acting—but Max didn't mind that so much. He wasn't crazy about Ilan.

Josh decided to give in to the inevitable, too, to wave the white flag of surrender and give himself a chance to grow into his body. He started looking into college prep courses.

Only Alex, Brandon, Rob, and Peter were left of the old guard. Peter and Rob were on their way to stardom. No worries there. Brandon had his evaluation before Max and learned that he had made it into Advanced. Alex got favorable notices too. Then it was Max's turn. He was sure it was going to be good news; it just had to be good news. Mrs. Gleboff called him to the inner sanctum. There was no need for him to speak—a good thing too. He couldn't have said a word if he'd had to; his voice was buried somewhere deep among the butterflies in his belly.

"Well, Max," began the director. She talked about his feet and his knees and his back; she talked about his injuries and all the classes he had left unfinished or had missed completely. He couldn't believe his ears. This couldn't be happening. He had expected to hear how pleased they were with his progress, with his seriousness, with his promise. He had expected to be told once again what a good dancer he was. Instead Mrs. Gleboff said that his attitude seemed improved but that it was still not quite up to snuff. Then she said that it had been his teachers' decision to give him a chance to show them that he really did want to dance and that he could take Advanced barre. Only the barre, she said, adding that he would have to sit and watch when the center work began and that his center work would have to be done in Intermediate, that it was in Intermediate where he would actually do his dancing. Then, after he proved to them all that he really did want to dance and to take it seriously, he could become a full member of Advanced—then and only then.

At first Max thought he would faint; his worst case had come true. A fifth year in Intermediate was what they had banished him to, he thought. In fact, they were giving him a chance, were not banishing him but merely asking him to think about whether he really wanted to do this thing called ballet, but he didn't see it that way. Once he knew he wasn't going to faint, he wanted to sob, to cry and cry and cry, and to tell Mrs. Gleboff how hurt he was, how desperately he wanted to be with the Advanced men instead of the Intermediate boys, how he just couldn't stand the humiliation of showing his face in that five-thirty class one more time. Then he felt like hitting her, just the way he had hit Josh a year ago, only harder. He was furious. "I'm so sick of that goddamn place," he said later. "I'm so sick of having to kiss ass, of having to have a smile on my face and prove things to them every minute of the day. I can dance better than half those guys in Advanced!"

Max even took his case to Mr. Rapp, and that's when he found that the teacher had recommended that he be promoted. That made him even angrier and more depressed. He went off to Heather Watts and Saratoga, but he came home within a week. He said that they treated him like a child there, that all the other students were twelve and thirteen years old, and that he was expected to follow rules designed for the younger kids. His mother said he missed the city.

Max's mother was philosophical about his future. "I'm very satisfied with his evaluation," she said, "and I'm sure he'll be allowed to take Advanced center. Saying he can't is just Gleboff. She doesn't like Max, but I know that Mr.

Martins does, so why should I care about her? And besides, the New York City Ballet isn't the only company in the world. I even prefer some of the other companies, where they do the romantic story ballets. Europe might be a good place for Max, perhaps Switzerland. If he joins one of the smaller companies, I'd rather he go to one in Europe, instead of, say, Kansas City. I feel I'd have to go with him, of course, and I'd much rather live in Europe than Kansas City."

Max didn't know where he wanted to dance. He sure wasn't going to go to some third-rate place, though, and to him Kansas City was definitely third-rate. Europe might be okay, but Europe would have to mean London or Paris, someplace everyone knew about. Max was after fame; he wasn't going to bury himself someplace where he couldn't have it. His major fantasy centered on winning a big international ballet competition and acquiring instant fame—"But one that is lasting," he always said. Then he would think about being in Intermediate or about his newest pain, and he'd wince. At those times Max thought it just might be better to give up ballet, to become a geologist like his father, or to have some kind of job working with kids. He liked kids, and they liked him too. He felt like one himself most of the time, and youngsters responded to him. If he were a geologist or a teacher, or even an architect, if he had a "normal" job, he thought, he could have a "normal" life. He wouldn't have to give up so much; he wouldn't have to be so single-minded, so disciplined and directed, and he wouldn't have to hurt all the time, either. He'd also never have to set his foot in Intermediate again, or look at Mrs. Gleboff, or watch his friends do better than he. Sometimes it sounded really good.

Until he took a "real" job, after he came home from Saratoga. Every night for the rest of the summer Max worked in a restaurant, as a busboy and a helper in the back of the bar.

He went to work at five in the afternoon and came home at five in the morning. Seven days a week. He slept all day, so he had no life outside his work life. He made less than minimum wage, and he had to do all the nastiest work, the things that the professional waiters didn't want to do. He hated it more than he had ever hated anything. "It was the worst summer of my life," he recalls. "Sometimes, in the early-morning hours, I would sit down on the stairs in the back of the restaurant and just tell myself, 'I'm not a busboy. I'm not a busboy. I'm not a barback. I'm a dancer.' "

And then it was September, time for SAB to start up again. Max got ready to take his first Advanced barre, and he tried not to think about what would happen when it was over. Still, a feeling of dread built up in his stomach. That first day, though, as the boys got ready to meet Stanley in Studio 3, all dread disappeared. Max had grown another inch; he was almost 5′6″, and he had stretched out carefully. He was even dressed properly, exclusively in black and white, no sweats, and he had remembered to leave his watch in his locker. He was seventeen, and he felt great, as though he owned the room. Finally he was taking his rightful place among the dancers of promise. He almost floated up to the barre, and he worked harder than he had ever worked in his life.

The thirty minutes flew by, and suddenly it was time for the center work. Max was not asked to join. He had to separate himself from the others, but he couldn't leave the room and hide his anguish. Again his humiliation was totally public. He had to sit and watch. After coming so close, he had to surrender his place and his pride—in front of everyone. Once again he was smaller than he thought, than he believed, than he wanted to be. "It was harsh," he says softly, shuddering, his face taking on the look of a scared little boy.

Epilogue

After the spring Workshop three SAB boys were taken into the New York City Ballet: Ben Huys from Belgium; Nilas Martins from Denmark; and Gordon Stevens from Nebraska. Jerry Kipper was named an apprentice. By fall new students had arrived at SAB from all over America, and a third outstanding Japanese boy was imported from Tokyo. Peter, Rob, and Phil Neal joined Jerry as front-row dancers in Stanley's class, the boys who get the most attention, the most outstanding of the students. Alex looked stronger than ever, and Josh came back, after all, for one more year. "It'll look good on my record," he says. "That's why I'm still here. But don't tell *them* that."

By October, Max had received permission from Stanley to stay for the full Advanced class, and by the end of that month, he felt secure enough to tie a forbidden sweatshirt around his waist, the only boy in the class to do so. He also took Intermediate every day, and adagio and social dancing, worked for Charlie, and went to PCS. He had been failing two of his subjects the previous spring, but he was able to convince his teachers to pass him, anyhow, so Max was actually on his way to high-school graduation—or at least to his junior year. Whether he would ever actually become a Poet of Gesture was still in question. "Now," he says, "for the first time I can really feel the limits of my body. I can understand what it is Stanley wants us to do, but I just can't make my body do it. Next May I'll be eighteen—old enough to go to war. I've lost so much time fooling around here. I just hope I can make it up."

In January, Sean Lavery underwent an exceedingly dangerous seven-and-a-half-hour operation to remove a benign tumor from his spinal column. The surgery was successful, and after a month in the hospital he set about learning to walk all over again, working with physical therapists and by himself with a dancer's amazing devotion and discipline. Says Lavery, "This has really put things in perspective. To think that just a few months ago I was worrying about casting and what was said to me in class. You know," he adds, "not once during all this have I said 'Boo hoo, why me?' Maybe I'm crazy, but I'm just working at getting back."

Acknowledgments

My thanks to the teachers and staff of the School of American Ballet for their friendly welcome and gracious assistance, to Lincoln Kirstein for making it all possible in the first place, to my husband, Sandy Padwe, for his wise and gentle ways, to my editor, Upton Brady, for always saying the right thing at the right time, and to all the many dancers and student dancers who shared their thoughts and experiences with me and who made my work a joy. May their careers be long and blessed, their injuries few, and their pirouettes pure poetry.

In my research for the historical part of this book, the Dance Collection of the New York Public Library was an invaluable source. The following books were also of great aid:

Richard Buckle. *Nijinsky*. New York, Simon & Schuster, 1971.

John Gregory and Alexander Ukladnikov. *Leningrad's Ballet: Maryinsky to Kirov*. New York, Universe, 1982.

Camilla Jessel, *Life at the Royal Ballet School*. New York, Methuen, Inc., 1979.

Lincoln Kirstein. *Thirty Years/The New York City Ballet*. New York, Alfred A. Knopf, 1978.

Joan Lawson. *A History of Ballet and Its Makers*. London, Dance Books, 1973.

Deryck Lynham. *Ballet Then and Now, A History of the Ballet in Europe*. London, Sylvan Press, 1947.

Peter Martins with Robert Cornfield. *Far from Denmark*. Boston, Little, Brown and Company, 1982.

Barbara Newman. *Striking a Balance, Dancers Talk About Dancing*. Boston, Houghton, Mifflin Company, 1982.

John Percival. *Nureyev, Aspects of the Dancer*. New York, G. P. Putnam's Sons, 1975.

Richard Philip and Mary Whitner. *Danseur, The Male in Ballet*. New York, Rutledge Books, 1977.

Gennady Smakov. *Baryshnikov, From Russia to the West*. New York, Farrar, Straus & Giroux, 1981.

Cobbett Steinberg. *San Francisco Ballet, The First Fifty Years*. San Francisco, San Francisco Ballet Association, 1983.

Bernard Taper. *Balanchine, A Biography*. New York, Times Books, 1984.

Walter Terry. *Great Male Dancers of the Ballet*. New York, Anchor Press/Doubleday, 1978.

Walter Terry. *The King's Ballet Master, A Biography of Denmark's August Bournonville*. New York, Dodd, Mead & Company, 1979.